Praise

"This incredible book holds the key to learning how to take risks and lead with courageous confidence. I want to be bold like Bolanle, and I know you will too."
 — **Meaghan B Murphy,** Editor in Chief of *Woman's Day* and author of *Your Fully Charged Life: A radically simple approach to having endless energy and filling every day with YAY*

"Bolanle generously breaks down her remarkable journey into a 'playbook' that readers will reference time and again. Whether it's your business, career or personal life, *Build Boldly* will inspire you to consider what success looks like for you and immediately get to work!"
 — **Ugonna Ibe-Ejiogu,** Creative Director, Cinnamon Lagos

"*Build Boldly* provides the reader with a clear narrative, outstanding practical to-dos and a level of personal encouragement that is not often found in traditional leadership material. Bola has illuminated **BOLD** in a way that the reader can't help but jump up and move forward!"
 — **Ted Maziejka,** Consultant

D0814158

"In this honest and open book, Bolanle Williams-Olley creates a judgment-free zone where one can be truly reflective of one's career journey and milestones so far, and get practical advice and tools to excel, starting from the job interview phase and throughout one's career. No work situation is perfect, and Williams-Olley uses her own experiences to show us how we too can not only survive our career, but expertly navigate different organizational cultures, build relationships and make bold moves to accomplish every goal we set for ourselves, and thrive. Every nugget in this book is gold, and you will find yourself bookmarking pages and returning to read them over and over again."

— **Odichinma Akosionu, MPH, PhD**
candidate—University of Minnesota School of Public Health

BUILD
BOLDLY

BOLANLE WILLIAMS-OLLEY

BUILD BOLDLY

CHART YOUR (UNIQUE) CAREER PATH
AND LEAD WITH COURAGE

Re think

First published in Great Britain in 2021
by Rethink Press (www.rethinkpress.com)

© Bolanle Williams-Olley

*This book is dedicated to **you**
as you boldly build what's next*

Contents

Foreword   1

Introduction   5
  Who this book is for   8
  BEING B.O.L.D.   10

1 Be Open To Many Paths   13
  Bold Move #1: Showing up as myself   14
  Bold Move #2: Defining a vision for myself   16
  Bold Move #3: Making a new place for myself   19
  BEING B.O.L.D.   22

2 Push Into Your Potential   23
  Exploring new interests   23
  A new approach to interviewing   26
  Setting myself up to succeed   27
  Defining my role   29
  Activating my potential   30
  BEING B.O.L.D.   32

3 The Power Of Visibility 33

Be memorable 34

Learning from other leaders 35

My turn to take the stage 37

Back to my roots 41

Lifting people up 42

BEING B.O.L.D. 44

4 Find Your Courage 45

The courage to begin 46

The courage to be yourself 48

Finding the courage to make tough decisions 49

BEING B.O.L.D. 55

5 Make New Rules 57

Leadership 58

Promotions 60

Annual reviews 61

Sharing the vision 63

Taking care of employees 65

BEING B.O.L.D. 68

6 Transparency 69

Understand why you're sharing 72

Transparency opens doors 74

The ripple effects of transparency 76

Transparency at work 78

BEING B.O.L.D. 83

7 Be Generous   **85**

Giving back   86

Expanding my impact   87

Generosity at work   92

Go and give   95

BEING B.O.L.D.   97

8 Build Community   **99**

Building a community as you build
your career   100

Build a community at your organization   104

Foster new connections   107

BEING B.O.L.D.   111

9 Your Legacy Starts Now   **113**

Legacy starts early   114

Vision and values   115

Take steps toward your dreams   117

Achieving your goals   119

My vision for the future   124

BEING B.O.L.D.   129

10 How To Be A B.O.L.D. Leader   **131**

Be yourself   132

Open your mind to new definitions
and opportunities   134

Lift others   137

Don't wait. Do it now   139

My leadership challenge to you   142

Conclusion   **143**

What I hope for you   145

B.O.L.D. Bonus: Ten prompts to help
you build boldly   147

Acknowledgements   **151**

The Author   **153**

Foreword

Yay! This incredible book holds the key to learning how to take risks and lead with courageous confidence. My friend Bolanle calls her secret sauce "building boldly" and her strategies are something I've been thinking about a lot lately as the new editor in chief of *Woman's Day* magazine. I take my role seriously and, with the example of bold leaders like Bolanle, I try really hard to practice fierce leadership. To me, that means lifting others up as I rise—growing together.

My True North at the helm has always been remembering that it's the "who" of the work that matters most. *Woman's Day* is "destination celebration." We give our 11 million readers an excuse to put fun on the calendar, but we're not exactly curing cancer. That's the point: it's never the "what" of the job that counts. It's the **who**. My team matters most.

I ask myself daily, "How can I make work more fun? Am I doing everything to ensure my staff feels 'tucked in' and safe? Who needs a pat on the back or more flexibility? Are we going the extra mile for milestones and recognizing achievements? Is everyone being treated equally whether they work in the mailroom or the C-suite? Do they feel they are being recognized?" Asking and proactively answering these questions ensures a healthy work environment.

In my book, *Your Fully Charged Life*, I dedicated an entire chapter to the idea that work is a microcosm of life. The same things that make us happy outside of the office (such as kudos, respect, purpose) will make us happy inside of the office. That's the kind of place I want to work in, and Bolanle is the kind of power-house I want to align with.

We first met in Detroit at the Mother Honestly Summit in 2019 and instantly connected. We'd traveled all the way to Michigan to learn we lived only two towns away in New Jersey. I skeptically invited her to join me for a 5:15 a.m. workout, and when she actually showed up (that's a 4 a.m. wakeup; I've been stood up more times than I can count!), I knew she was one of my people.

Bolanle is a woman who is true to her word and guiding principles. I want to be bold like Bolanle, and I know you will too. I hope you use this book as an example for making your own decisions at work. We all need mentors and examples—people who are blazing trails ahead of us.

The next generation needs those examples too. This is a book I'll be proud to share one day soon with my tween daughter. I want to be certain that she has strong, powerful women guiding and leading her and showing her the way.

My challenge to you: as you read this book, look for examples and ideas you can apply to your own life and work to be your boldest, most fully-charged self.

Meaghan B. Murphy, Editor in Chief of *Woman's Day* and author of *Your Fully Charged Life: A radically simple approach to having endless energy and filling every day with YAY.*

Introduction

I'm Bolanle; some people call me Bola. I'm part-owner at Mancini Duffy, where I oversee the financial performance of an architecture and interior design firm in New York City with a 100+-year history.

In the last few years alone, I have made huge leaps in my career. Looking back now, I can see that my path so far has been all about **relationships, curiosity** and **taking bold action**.

I was born and raised in Lagos, Nigeria, as an only child to a single mother who modeled the value of **relationships**. No matter what someone's title or position was—whether they were a bus driver or a CEO—my mom made sure she took the time to get to know them, treat them with respect and help them as well as she could. Observing her played a huge role for me in terms of how I relate with people and form relationships.

When I'd go to her office, I'd see how she ran her group in her work life as a financial controller. Even when I was seven years old, I could tell this lady led things. Later, she became an entrepreneur and worked hard to build her business. Seeing her entrepreneurial side made me **curious** early on. Because of her, I was always starting businesses. In high school, I sold Valentine's cards. In college, I crocheted earrings and sold them on campus. Thanks to my mom, I have always had a curious spirit to learn new things and understand how they are done.

However, even with my drive and curiosity, I didn't always lean fully into the bold side of myself. In college, I was timid in professional settings. I put myself into a box. I knew I wanted to study mathematics, but I wasn't confident about how math would translate into a career. I couldn't always present myself well because I wasn't being myself.

My pivotal moment happened when I found my courage and boldness during an interview for my first job. I made the decision to take ownership of my degree, accept who I am, be proud of the things I had accomplished and speak about the value that I, as a twenty-one-year-old, could bring to the organization.

I vocalized clearly who I am and what I'm looking for. I started **taking bold action**, making confident, courageous decisions that have led me to where I am today.

Over the next fourteen years of my career, I focused on relationships, stayed curious and open to learning and improving, and wrote my own bold playbook with an eye on new opportunities. Now, as a leader, I get to make bold decisions to support my team. Together, we have a shared vision of how we want to perform, to show up for the larger organization and ourselves.

For me, part of being bold is finding ways to create solutions and make an impact—not sometime in the future, but *now*. When I was a kid, that meant helping my friends. Now, I'm always asking myself, "How can I have an impact in my immediate realm *and* the larger realm? Once I have knowledge, how can I pour that back out to help other folks with the same pain points and problems as I had?"

My answer has been to look inward to make changes in my team and company, but I also look outward and start organizations outside of my day job to help other people in my own way:

- I started **SheBuildsLives** to improve education in Nigeria. Through one project at a time, we provide resources and opportunities to children living in low-income communities.

- **SheBuildsWaves** started when I got into a position of leadership and decided to help other women who were coming up in my industry. I wanted to have conversations about how we can show up as our full selves and make waves in our careers and beyond. I wanted to show other women that if I could become a chief financial officer (CFO) after coming from Nigeria as an immigrant, maybe they could achieve their wildest dreams too.

- **SheBuildsMoney** helps small firms work through struggles managing their finances. I said to myself, "I've spent fourteen years in finance. Rather than waiting until later, how can I create resources and tools to help owners of small businesses right now so that they stay in business and get to do the things they love?"

I'm always thinking about how I can make it easier for someone else who is just starting out, unsure or struggling. I'm a serial solution-seeker. Sharing more, collaborating more and giving more information can only help all of us move up together.

Who this book is for

If I've learned anything in my career, it's that taking **bold** action is the fastest way to fully be yourself and create exponential growth. When I was starting out, I couldn't have predicted that my career would grow as quickly as it has. I didn't picture myself in a leadership role.

Even though I'm still in the middle of my career, I'm ready to share my journey and lessons with you. I wrote this book to encourage others to take bigger and bolder steps. So many people just need an extra push. After reading this book, I hope you will say, "I can do it. I'm up for the task. I can lean into my potential."

Do you need a nudge to take action? Are you ready to take a big, bold step to:

- **Change your path?**
  You're ready to make a jump in your career and write your own playbook. You're ready to grow.

- **Change the path for others?**
  As a leader, you're ready to change how things are done in your team or office. You want to challenge the status quo, take a chance on your co-workers and build an environment that nurtures people to be their best. You're ready to help others grow.

Let's say to ourselves, "I may not know everything, but I'm going to bet on myself and see what happens." Let's get rid of the fear and start showing up as who we are. Let's all craft our own playbooks.

BEING B.O.L.D.

To help us make bigger decisions, we need to think about being **B.O.L.D.** The acronym stands for:

Be yourself
The moment I started really being myself, good things happened. Leaning into my most authentic self has propelled me to where I am now. Understand who you are. Know your strengths and amplify what makes you unique and powerful. Don't be afraid to be yourself.

Open your mind to new definitions and opportunities
My journey has taught me that we should challenge the status quo. Just because things have always been done one way doesn't mean that's the best way. How can you push yourself and others to think beyond old definitions and limits? How can you push against boundaries and explore new ways of thinking and working to unlock new opportunities? Open your mind, open doors and seize those opportunities.

Lift others
When people see my nonprofit work, they sometimes ask how I have time to think beyond the daily demands of my job and family. My reply is that we all have time to lift others up with us. Once you start exercising the muscle of thinking about

other people, it will expand. Find ways to lift others, starting with the people you work with.

Don't wait—do it now
There will never be a "perfect" time to do anything. We don't know what will happen tomorrow, so why wait? If there are changes you want to make in your career, start now. How can you make progress today? If you aren't feeling fulfilled, how can you take charge? If there are changes you want to make as a leader, start now. Take one step at a time.

Are you ready to be **B.O.L.D.** and create your own playbook? Are you ready to bring the people around you up with you?

You are?

That's awesome! Let's start right away.

1
Be Open To Many Paths

When you're at the beginning of your career, it can feel like there's one specific defined path you're supposed to follow. You pick a major, you get a job in that field, you do the tasks in the job description and you keep your head down. All you have to do is get on the right path and you'll be set.

I learned early in my career that real life is a lot messier than that. To me, the key to growing and thriving is the opposite of "keeping your head down"—it's about exploring different paths, finding new interests, working on a variety of projects and learning from all of the people around you. If you're not open to testing different paths, then you'll box yourself in early on—and boxing yourself in is not to your advantage.

I have found over and over again that I'm most fulfilled and successful when I stay open to many possible paths and make bold moves when I see an opportunity.

Bold Move #1: Showing up as myself

In college, I studied math. I applied for a couple of internships, but they didn't come through; my interviews just didn't click, so I kept working on my degree, including a master's thesis in fluid dynamics. I had studied impressive subjects, but I didn't have any real work experience—and I had no idea how to talk about my math degree in job interviews.

When I got to my senior year, the clock was ticking. As an international student, I knew that if I wanted to stay in the United States and get work experience, I needed to find a job and a company to sponsor me. I worked through career services at my school, considered teaching and even thought about going for a Ph.D.

A lot of my friends were getting jobs in accounting, so I applied for financial services programs, but again, the interviews weren't clicking. I didn't have the lingo or the knowledge; I would prepare for the interviews, but because I wasn't in my comfort zone, I would mess up. Nervous and easily thrown off course, I tried to fit a mold—to be the cookie-cutter candidate that fit what employers were looking for—but even that backfired. Although the interview might have gone well and I thought I'd done all I needed to, I didn't get the job.

I started to wonder, "Why isn't this working for me?"

One day, I was sitting in the computer lab at school, and on a whim, I looked for jobs in the *New York Times* classifieds, stumbling on a posting for a junior project accountant at an architectural firm. I didn't think I wanted to do accounting—that had been my mother's path and I wanted to do something different—but a technical drawing class I had taken in high school had left me with an interest in architecture. Even though I had no clue what a junior project accountant did, I applied for the position and got called for an interview.

That interview was the pivotal moment that changed everything for me. I had to try something different, so I took my first bold step and decided to show up as myself, communicating the value I could bring to the job. After all, I had nothing to lose.

When I got to the interview, everything clicked into place. The person sitting across from me had also studied math and we immediately connected about that. I had never talked about my thesis in an interview, but he wanted to know all about it. All of a sudden, my math degree became my differentiator. He was genuinely interested in me, my work and where I was from. I was comfortable and relaxed.

Best of all, I got the job.

I couldn't have been more elated. That was such a proud moment—I had finally made my studies work for me, and I'd done it by being myself.

Bold Move #2: Defining a vision for myself

I started my first job as a junior project accountant in New York City in 2007, and for the first year, I spent my time learning. What did it mean to do accounting in an architectural firm? What did it mean to be a project accountant?

Sometimes, I felt unsure when I talked to my college friends who were all working in financial services at accounting firms. It was hard for me to communicate what I did. Their roles seemed more clearly defined than mine, but I continued to focus on learning as much as I could at my new job.

Then the 2008 financial crisis happened. New York's architectural industry was flattened. Less cash was coming into the company and layoffs were inevitable. The first person to go was the senior project accountant who had hired me. The next people were the two project accountants above me. As the youngest (and probably the cheapest) employee in the group, I kept my job.

I had a decision to make: I could put my head down and just be thankful I had a job, or I could look for an opportunity in the difficult times we were all experiencing. That's when I made my second bold move.

I went to the CFO of the company and said, "We've lost these people, but I'm willing to pick up the extra work. I can do it as I'm open to learning about everything they were doing. Please take a chance on me."

The CFO said yes. He then went on to mentor me, helping me create new processes. We would sit down over lunch and work through tough projects, then he gave me assignments and feedback. In other words, he invested in me.

As the CFO gave me more and more responsibility, by the end of 2008, I was supporting sixteen project managers, doing the billing for our New York and Los Angeles offices, and all of the month-end accounting. Learning how accounting supported the firm's incredible projects, I made sure they were financially successful.

That year was a time of major growth for me. Instead of working toward someone else's vision of success, I turned inward and defined my own vision. It was time to quiet the noise and focus on being the best I could be in my position. How could I make myself a valuable asset to the team? How could I contribute?

I didn't just see myself as an accountant. Instead of keeping my head down and running the numbers, I let my curiosity lead, asking, "What are we doing there? What is this project is about?"

My background in math had taught me to question things. I had a different approach to solving problems, asking project managers the right questions to get them thinking. By staying curious and building relationships, I became a strategic partner.

During that long and challenging year, I saw the benefit of exploring multiple paths. Even though I was technically a junior project accountant, I took advantage of an unfortunate situation to learn about various parts of the group, ask new questions, explore new solutions and understand my own strengths.

Looking back, I appreciate the CFO's generous leadership. He saw the knowledge gap between what I knew as a twenty-two-year-old accountant and what I wanted to know, sharing his knowledge with me and helping me build a strong foundation. This continues to serve as an example for me as I help others build their own strong foundations.

I was able to refine my vision and set myself on a new path. If I was going to keep learning from experience, though, I needed a different experience, which meant working at a different firm.

It was time for me to move on.

Bold Move #3: Making a new place for myself

I had gotten comfortable at my first company. My coworkers were like family to me: we ate lunch together and the atmosphere was human and friendly. When I handed in my resignation, I felt anxious and apprehensive.

When I walked into my first day at my new firm, I knew everything would be different there. The company was, and still is, one of the largest and most influential architecture, design, engineering and urban planning firms in the world. Its name carries weight and it has a reputation for impressive projects.

But the culture was vastly different than what I'd experienced at my old firm. For one, the company had double the number of employees in its New York office alone. It was a big well-oiled machine, but in a company that large, it can be easy to get lost in the numbers.

Even though I felt the difference, I was willing to put in the work and learn. I knew that having a prestigious company's name on my résumé would be a catalyst for good things to happen later in my career. However, instead of learning from a mentor like I had at my first job, I had to figure a lot out on my own. My manager was the New York office controller who had responsibility for seven other project accountants in addition to me, so she was extremely busy.

There wasn't any room for me to expand my role. I wouldn't be able to grow there. This time, my bold move was doubling down on relationships. Instead of learning from the existing culture, I built my own culture by forming meaningful relationships. Focusing on the people around me, I got to know the project managers. Staying curious, I kept asking questions. The project managers I worked with saw the value of an accountant who was constantly working with them throughout the month and raising flags before they became issues.

Continuing to show up as myself at work, I started bringing in hats that I had crocheted to donate to children's hospitals. I talked about my side projects, my nonprofit work and my life outside of the office. By being myself, I was able to form relationships with even the most closed-off personalities. Suddenly, I wasn't just the girl who worked in accounting; I was Bola who crochets hats for sick babies.

When you work somewhere that's impersonal, being yourself is like a shot of real life. People welcome it and are drawn to it, even those who are notoriously prickly or hard to work with. There may be times in your career when you're not culturally aligned with your employer or colleagues, but there's still a lot you can learn. You just have to be willing to create your own path.

BEING B.O.L.D.

Here's what I learned from my early career experiences about building boldly:

Be yourself
If you're trying to fit into someone else's mold, they'll never see you for who you are. Forget finding the one "right" path and start carving your own, based on your strengths and interests.

Open your mind to new definitions and opportunities
Keep your head up. Look for the projects, people and ideas that draw you in. Ask questions. Don't stop learning and wondering.

Lift others
My first boss taught me the value of investing in others. He gave me the generous gift of his time and trust. Now, my goal as a leader is to help others learn, grow and lean into their full potential.

Don't wait—do it now
I knew that I had to take charge of my career and proactively seek out new opportunities. I could have stayed in my first job for years, but I took a bold step toward learning and growing.

2
Push Into Your Potential

One of the true joys of my career so far has been understanding my own potential and the potential of the people around me. Work is much more rewarding when you're pushing yourself to be your best and helping others do the same.

Exploring new interests

It was after working for ten years, I realized I needed to make a change to push to the next level of my career journey. During my first decade in work, I was also moving into the next phase of my personal life as a mother, nonprofit leader and graduate student. I started SheBuildsLives to improve education for children in low-income communities in Nigeria. I also had a baby and had to learn the balancing act of being a working parent.

I remember one of the worst moments in my first year as a working mom; I'd already taken the day after Christmas off, since I didn't have childcare that day, and in January, I asked for another day off for my daughter's first birthday. The answer I got from my manager was unequivocal:

"You take too much time off for your daughter."

I went to the bathroom and bawled. I'd tried my best to do good work for the company, but at that moment, I needed something different, so I thought about what might come next for me. I had been working in the architecture world for ten years, forming relationships and learning everything I could. Should I pivot out of the industry? Was it time to make a career switch?

In typical Bolanle fashion, I decided to explore more. I had an interest in education, which had driven me to start SheBuildsLives, and I wanted to learn more, so I looked for programs where I could apply my math degree and accounting experience to education. The perfect match for me was at New York University (NYU) with its education and social policy program.

Having applied to NYU and got in, I found out I was pregnant with my second child. I started graduate school six months pregnant as a full-time working mom, but I knew my job wasn't going to give me any flexibility, so I took all of my classes at night.

Midway through my degree course, I had a crisis of doubt. I didn't know what to do next. How was I going to make this all work? It felt like I needed to do something drastic—change industries or start over in a new career—but I had two kids under two. It didn't seem like an ideal time to make a big career move. How could I? I didn't want to have to explain to a new employer about the demands on my time and prove myself as a good worker all over again.

That was when I had a pivotal conversation with my husband, who encouraged me and helped me reframe my situation. He told me to keep pressing forward and finish my degree, even if I didn't have a specific plan for what would come next. His belief in me helped me see that I didn't have to start over. I was working hard and moving in the right direction, and good things would come.

And he was right.

A new approach to interviewing

A former coworker, Christian Giordano, had recently become president and majority shareholder of Mancini Duffy, an architecture and design firm with a 100+-year history in New York. He wanted to meet with me, tell me more about his vision for the firm's next generation and interview me for the role of controller.

Ten years after my initial job interviews, I had a completely different approach. I went in ready for an open, honest, transparent conversation. I was going to be myself and advocate for myself. I knew what I could offer, my value, strengths and weaknesses. With my passion and drive, I knew what I wanted to accomplish. And I knew what I needed to do to push myself into my full potential.

In addition to that, I was clear about my concerns. If I was going to move into a leadership role, I wanted my values and the firm's values to be aligned. And it was time to hold out for the things that were important to me—in my case, the flexibility I needed as a mom of two with interests and priorities outside of work.

I asked outright at the interview, "What are your company's policies around family?" And I talked about my degree program. Would there be any issues concerning my work as a graduate student? It was bold of me to lay all my cards out at the interview, but if I was going to take this position, I needed to see myself growing there.

In response, I was met with interest about my life beyond my primary job function. My former colleague, now my interviewer, asked, "What is this degree? Tell me more about it. Tell me more about your nonprofit." Then he told me his vision for the firm. As majority stakeholder, he had been thinking about what kind of organization he wanted to set up, how he'd make sure the people who worked there had a good work-life balance. He was determined to make the historic firm less uptight and bring a new leadership approach. His vision was exciting to me and aligned with what I was looking for.

Setting myself up to succeed

Having made it clear exactly what I would need to succeed in the job, including support and mentorship, I left the interview feeling really good. I had communicated my skills well and had been myself. I got the job.

Because I'd been clear that I'd need specific support to learn how to do the job, I got it immediately. The firm hired a part-time financial consultant to mentor me during my first year. Having that formal support was a huge help in getting me up to speed fast.

Whether you're hiring a star performer right out of school or pulling someone up into their first leadership role, it's worth spending the time and money upfront to set them up to succeed—in other words, to make the impact you hired them to make. Help them close their knowledge gaps. It's always worth it. If you don't spend time and money on nurturing your new recruits, it will cost you in the long term. Why hire A players if you're not going to push into their potential to become A+ players?

HOW TO BE BOLD IN AN INTERVIEW

Miscommunication in interviews happens when people don't talk enough. Use the job interview process to clearly communicate what you expect from the working relationship. What will you bring, and what will the company do to support you?

Clear expectations are critical for both parties:

- **Know your value** and what you'd bring to the role, and be ready to express that. There's a reason you made it into the interview room, so start from a place of confidence.

- **Ask the hard questions.** Clearly state the parts of the job that make you hesitate. Ask how you'll be mentored and developed. How will you get the support you need to make the impact expected of you?

- **Look for leaders who will invest in you.** Ask yourself whether this company will help you push into your potential. The firm will always look out for itself, so you have to make sure you're looking out for yourself.

Defining my role

My first year at Mancini was all about learning. How did this 100+-year-old firm work? I would be taking the reins from a CFO who had been there for twenty years, and most of the staff in the group had also been there for decades. They'd always done things in a particular way.

I spent six months getting to know the firm, and then introduced my own ideas and experience. What could we change? How could we immediately set up the firm for financial success? How would we build the right relationships with external accountants and vendors to make sure the firm ran as it should? I gave my team room to experiment and change. If we put out a new policy and realized it wasn't working, we could always change it.

That year was a huge growing process for me, but I enjoyed it because I had a seat at the table and my voice was heard. My opinion was respected. I had a team to brainstorm with. And because I had blatantly been myself in my interview, I had the freedom to be myself on the job from Day One.

Even though I was technically a controller, I was really doing the work of a CFO. Because Mancini is a smaller firm than the ones I'd worked for previously, my role included exposure to different parts of the organization. I oversaw finance and accounting, human resources (HR), office operations and even some of IT, so I was able to touch everything. That's how I learned more about my strengths and weaknesses.

I was growing into a strategic role as CFO with many different functions under my purview, but I was also still managing the daily grind of accounting. I quickly identified the functions that I didn't have interest in or shouldn't be doing, and decided it was time for me to bring in support.

I ended up hiring an operations manager who is excellent. Her role as an organized, competent team member has been key to my development as a thriving CFO. Passing along some responsibilities to her helped me focus on my strengths and step into my role as a more strategic partner.

Activating my potential

After a year as the controller, it was time for me to take on the title that matched the work I was doing: CFO. When my title changed, I looked back on the past ten years and thought about how I'd gotten there. It was because I'd pushed into my potential. I'd put in the work to identify what I was great at and how I could bring more value to my employer, believing that I could not only do the work, but excel.

Activating your potential is exciting. You start to see the possibility—how you can build new skills and create real change. I realized how I could make a larger impact in the industry and beyond, pushing into my potential as a female leader and making my voice heard.

There are so many things that have made me believe in the concept of limitless possibilities. And Mancini, a company focused on doing things differently, has been a fertile learning ground for me. My experience has launched exponential growth—I'm now part-owner of the firm, able to open the door for other people's ideas, growth, exploration and possibilities.

Because I was supported to push into my potential, now I can empower others to push into their potential. And together, we can push the firm into its big, exciting, limitless potential.

When someone champions you, they move you into a position to champion others. My message to you: champion and be championed. Your career can seem like a solitary ladder—working your way to the top— but in the best cases, it's an interconnected web that you're weaving in community with others. Your rising tide can lift other boats, too.

BEING B.O.L.D.

Be yourself

If your current employment isn't aligned with your values and your family situation, it's probably time to move on. Remember to be yourself and advocate for yourself, even if it's years since you were last going for job interviews. Be sure to ask up front what support you will be given to thrive in your new role.

Open your mind to new definitions and opportunities

When you have grown as much as you can in one place, resist the temptation to stay with what you know. Get out of your comfort zone and go find those opportunities, and never stop looking for chances to learn.

Lift others

Whether you're hiring a new graduate or setting an established employee on the way to a leadership role, make sure they have all the support they need to succeed.

Don't wait—do it now

Excuses aren't reasons to delay; they're just excuses. Ignore them. Being a parent, for example, is no reason to stall your own progression.

3
The Power Of Visibility

"Visibility" is a concept that can be pretty invisible most of the time. However, when I reflect on my career so far, I realize that visibility—the people who I saw and the people who could see me—has had a major impact.

Who do you see above you in leadership positions? Whose job do you aspire to have? Do you see people who you can relate to? And who can see you? Who is watching you as an example?

There have been a few key moments in my working life that have helped me understand who I could be and what example I could leave behind for others. Let's explore how visibility has played a role in my career. As you're reading, continually ask yourself: "Who can I see?" and "Who can see me?"

Be memorable

When I look back at my early career, I can't claim that I was always acting with complete intention. Often, we only find the patterns and threads in hindsight, but while I can't say that I was on a mission to make myself visible, I did work to be memorable.

I made myself memorable through my everyday relationships at work. I treated people well, working hard to get to know them even in a culture that didn't prioritize relationships. Sometimes, I had to crack through a thick exterior to find the person inside.

The relationships I built have driven my career and opened up new opportunities for me. The power of strong relationships will never disappoint; it's always worth getting to know people and treating them in a way that will make them remember you. If you can't be visible, you can at least be memorable.

In my second job, the culture among my peers—the other accountants—was to stay in the back office, but that wasn't me. I was always out on the floor, talking to project managers and partners, looking for opportunities to help me expand and grow. It was my constant visibility—the push to be remembered and known—that landed me highly prestigious projects. Working on those projects created an opportunity for me to shine and stand out from the pack.

When you think about how to boost your visibility as an employee, it's all about speaking up for yourself and being in front of your bosses. Make yourself memorable. When you put yourself out there every day at work, the people in charge are more likely to remember you when it comes to assigning the next high-profile project.

Looking back, I realize that at some point, I made a decision. I wanted to grow in my career, so I made the decision to step into the light and be seen. I needed to make myself visible to the people who were making decisions about me behind closed doors. The fastest way to do that was to showcase myself.

It's not enough to just do good work, to "let your work speak for itself." You have to represent yourself.

Learning from other leaders

After becoming part-owner of Mancini, I was starting to feel a pull to help other women at work and build a community where women could share new examples of success and lift each other up. How could I have a larger impact on women in my industry? I wanted women to have a way to help each other along without hiding who we are. Human beings are all multifaceted and we are unlikely to bloom if we hide any part of ourselves.

I started a new organization, SheBuildsWaves. I think of it as a collective of women who make waves in their careers in the built environment. We meet online and in person, and I hope SheBuildsWaves will help women push for more inclusivity and visibility.

THE FORBES WOMEN'S SUMMIT

Through my work at SheBuildsWaves, I was invited to the 2019 Forbes Women's Summit, an event that really opened my eyes to my potential and the potential of all women at work by making our stories visible. I remember sitting in the crowd, surrounded by 250+ leaders and change makers who were opening doors, making progress and bringing others along with them. The energy, knowledge and inspiration I gained from the incredible panel of women sharing their stories and doing great things was life-changing.

For me, there were two big takeaways from sitting in that audience. One was the power of being relatable as you're progressing up the career ladder so that people can connect with your stories. The second was to always ensure other people, especially women, are given space and an opportunity to succeed and thrive.

Christine Lagarde, who was chair of the International Monetary Fund (IMF) and is now President of the European Central Bank, said that if she walks into a meeting and there aren't any women at the table, she walks out. But then, she also talked about getting manicures. That was so relatable to me—she does really tough work, but she was telling us stories that made her more human. I realized that she was so much more than her important role.

Another person I connected with was Anjali Sud, the CEO of the video platform Vimeo. Just a couple of years older than me, she had recently been promoted; even though she did not have prior leadership experience, she was given the opportunity to run this incredible organization.

When asked how her new role was going, she said, "I'm figuring it out as I go." I connected with that because I was doing the same in my leadership position: figuring it out and writing my own playbook. It was OK to be transparent about what I did and didn't know.

That event was confirming for me. I realized that I may have a fancy title, but that didn't strip me of the human side of how I should run my business or how I should approach my role.

My turn to take the stage

I was ready to get my name out more in my industry. Already in a position of leadership, I wanted to be known for who I really am. I wanted people to hear my story, realize what I am all about and the impact I am making, both at my firm and beyond.

I had started speaking at small events through my church. One of my first speaking engagements was for a group of teens and I got to share a bit more about my background. I told them how I'd gotten a non-traditional degree in math and made my own path for myself, showing them the possibilities they could explore.

This was when the power of the relationships I'd built started to pay me back, leading to more visibility. After I started SheBuildsWaves, I got the opportunity to be featured in a new magazine, *Madame Architect*, started by Julia Gamolina to fill a void in the industry. The magazine is "Dedicated to the built environment and to the empowerment, advancement, and visibility of the women who work in it." Julia was interested in featuring me since, as CFO, I had a different perspective than the architects and designers she had been featuring. When she interviewed me, she wanted to know about the "why" behind all of my work.

The article she wrote was called "Open Doors" and it was transformative for me. It exposed me to a wider audience of women, and men, in the industry. They got to know a little bit more about who I am, my passion projects and how I think about doing multiple things in parallel—not just climbing a ladder, but exploring different paths and pulling other people up with me. When that article was published, more people started reaching out.

A former colleague then connected me to Yiselle Santos, the founder of W.I.E.L.D. Your Story, a platform focused on visibility and engagement through storytelling. She invited me to share my story at her event, where I met a young lady who was planning the American Institute of Architects Women's Leadership Summit. The planning team wanted to revamp the event to include younger and more diverse voices. She gave me the opportunity to be on the main stage, speaking to 1,000 women.

In just a few years, I went from speaking to ten to twenty people at church group events to hundreds of women on a large national stage. Each opportunity led to another.

Whenever I walk on stage, I think back to my experience at the Forbes summit, where I'd been struck by the human side of powerful female leaders. I wanted to be the same kind of relatable, encouraging example for the women in the audience. The American Institute of Architects Women's Leadership Summit was full of women who were emerging in their careers, making shifts in their work or stepping into management positions.

Oddly enough, I didn't feel nervous. Nigerian weddings are often attended by 1,000 people and I had experienced tougher crowds—they don't come much tougher than teenagers in church at 9 a.m. on Sunday morning! Also, I felt calm because I knew who I was. I wasn't pretending to be someone I wasn't.

When you get on the big stages in front of hundreds of people, you trip up when you put on a front, so you have to lean further into your authentic self. The women in the crowd at the American Institute of Architects summit were all dealing with their own insecurities, just like I was. If they could connect or relate to me in some way, then my job would be done.

Afterwards, a lot of people came up to me. Part of their feedback was that they really appreciated how real I was. And even better, I continue to hear from women who were in the audience that day. The event ignited something in them. Women were inspired to go start their own projects and movements.

One told me, "I left that day feeling the need to act." I heard from a group who had started a podcast profiling women in the design and construction industry. Another started advocating for immigrant architects.

All of that because they saw women on stage making waves.

The lesson I learned: visibility is an invisible force, but it can drive major change and action.

Back to my roots

Ten years after my graduation, my college mentor died in a tragic accident. I had written a paper with him and learned a lot from him. He had a tough exterior, but I managed to break through it and get to know him.

I went to his funeral, and while I was there, I met the current chair of the math department. After talking to me for a while, he invited me to speak to the students about how I had used my math degree. He told me that my story would be inspiring, because few students in the applied math program actually apply their math knowledge—they end up either doing pure math or pursuing Ph.Ds. He wanted me to show them what was possible.

Later, I wrote an article about the lessons I'd learned from being CFO. The article made it to the current president of the college, and she invited me to join the business advisory board. By talking and sharing,

I was able to build new relationships and expand my impact.

Lifting people up

The next question was, what was I going to do with my newfound visibility? How was I going to use it to make an impact? For me, my visibility has never been about me. It's always been about acting from a position of service. I didn't want my legacy to be just about my own career progression; I wanted to help other people.

Being on those big stages made me more motivated to tackle big issues in my work. The women in the audience had questions about how to get paid fairly and how to approach their firms' leadership. Their questions inspired me to work harder on those problems.

I had big plans for 2020—it was going to be my year to get out there and continue to share my story. I wanted to craft my legacy and help other women, especially around the issues of the gender wage gap and getting more women into leadership positions.

But then, the pandemic hit and all of my original plans went out the window. I had to focus my attention on keeping my firm stable. Yet even in those stressful times, I wanted to keep making a broader impact as a financial leader.

I was able to launch a new impact organization to help with the specific challenges of this time. In the midst of a global pandemic, 2020 birthed SheBuildsMoney, which is designed to help small businesses be financially successful. In the architecture industry, 70% of firms are small. I wanted to create tools and resources that would help these one-, two- or three-person companies manage better and last longer.

Visibility can cause a ripple effect. You set an example; someone sees you and is inspired; they create more positive change and impact. I'm hopeful that the next generation of women are closely watching our example now and planning the ripples they'll make in the world.

When I became CFO of Mancini, my daughter was four years old. I remember her saying, "Mommy, are you the boss-boss now?" My daughter and other young black girls can see me, and they know it's possible to be a leader in any industry. They have a clear example. And I've experienced the power of having an example.

Take a few minutes now to ask yourself again, "Who can I see?" and "Who can see me?" The answers to those questions mean a lot.

BEING B.O.L.D.

Be yourself
When you find yourself on center stage, you might be tempted to act like whoever you think you're "supposed" to be. However, it's always better to drop the fake persona. Don't think about "should," just be who you really are. If you want people to truly see you, you have to be yourself.

Open your mind to new definitions and opportunities
You don't know what ripple effects you might cause. By stepping into the spotlight, you might inspire others to stand up, pursue their own path and create change. Act boldly and confidently, knowing that the ripples will follow.

Lift others
Time and again, I've discovered that helping others creates new connections, relationships, ideas and opportunities. If your goal is to be more visible, start by shining a light on the brightest people around you.

Don't wait—do it now
I could have waited for the "right" time to move into a leadership role or to start sharing my story, but there is no right time. If you have something to contribute or a story you want to tell, do it now.

4
Find Your Courage

What does it take to carve out a place for yourself at work? How do you boldly build a career? For a long time, I thought confidence was the most important piece of the puzzle. However, recently, I've realized before you can build your confidence, you have to build your courage.

It takes courage to put yourself out there—to go into a big interview and lay your cards on the table. It takes courage to be yourself. When I reflect back on the pivotal moments in my career when I had to make bold decisions, I realize that I called on my inner courage every time.

I built my courage when I owned my math degree and really leaned into that skill. When I decided to be myself in job interviews and speak my value, most importantly in my interview with Mancini. At that point in my career, I needed to work for a firm that aligned with my values and perspective. I needed to understand where the firm was going and how I would fit into that future, so I spoke candidly about my family, my priorities and my knowledge gap. And once I got the job, I took my seat at the leadership table and voiced my opinions.

Each of those moments took courage. And my courage has built up over time. These days, I'm not nervous to speak up or say what's on my mind because I have been practicing—flexing my courage muscle—for years. I finally have the courage to be confident.

The courage to begin

"If you have the courage to begin, you have the courage to succeed."
—David Viscott

I always keep this quote from David Viscott in the back of my mind. At many times in my career, and as I have built my side projects, I've needed courage just to get started.

When you face a big opportunity, you can choose to shrink down into your comfort zone, or have the courage to take the first step into the unknown. I can point to so many times when I was taking on something big, new or overwhelming. I wasn't sure what all of the steps would look like, but I have learned that if I get started, the additional steps will unfold.

I commit to really big, bold goals, tackling them by breaking them into much smaller bite-sized pieces. By getting started, I can progress toward my end goal. This habit probably comes from my math background. It's literally how to solve complex math problems—one line at a time. It's a methodology that has helped me succeed over and over again.

For example, when I start a new project with SheBuilds-Lives, I have to summon the courage to raise funds to execute it. However, as soon as I make the first phone call, the next steps will come. When I became CFO, if I had just looked at the title and the scope of the role and all the responsibility that came with it, I would have been completely overwhelmed. But I've progressed by dealing with problems and situations as they come in little pieces. Even writing this book took courage to get started. I knew I wanted to do it, but I didn't know all of the steps I'd take from the beginning to the end.

There's always going to be a moment of fear. When you feel afraid, unsure, like going back into your comfort zone, call on that courage muscle and push through. Somebody, somewhere is going to benefit from it. Taking the first step means you're already succeeding.

The courage to be yourself

"Sometimes just being yourself is the radical act. When you occupy space in systems that weren't built for you, your authenticity is your activism." —Elaine Welteroth

Being myself—in my industry, in my role, in my firm— is an act of courage. When I think about the spaces that I have occupied, when I have been courageous and authentic, I've grown. It is true what Elaine Welteroth says in the quote that begins this section: being ourselves is a radical act, it is activism. In moments when I didn't have the courage and decided to shrink back, my career stagnated.

When you lean in to be yourself, you'll see fruitful outcomes that will help you grow or learn. If you never push yourself out of your comfort zone, you won't learn about your own strengths and passions, and you won't grow in your career.

Even before I joined Mancini, the president was developing an authentic brand for the company. He is committed to creating an employee-centric culture based on a simple principle: "We put our people first; our people put our clients first." That value shows up in the firm's work and in how it represents itself in public.

When I was interviewing for my job, I scrolled through Mancini's social media and what I saw impressed me greatly. I saw profiles of employees, including a long-time office services employee who was universally loved by his coworkers. I saw the *people* behind the projects; you can't get to know much about what it's like to work at a firm by looking at pictures of buildings. Mancini was shining a light on its people, a courageous decision that, at least in my case, paid off.

Be uniquely, courageously yourself. Then you will align with bold companies and clients, creating the future you really want.

Finding the courage to make tough decisions

A lot of my reflection about courage has happened in the past few years, as I have stepped into my leadership role as CFO and part-owner of Mancini. Running a firm, both from the financial perspective and in terms of my responsibility to employees and their families, takes a lot of courage. Along with other C-suite people, I have to make bold, difficult decisions that move the firm where we want it to go. Those decisions require me to flex my courage muscle fully.

The courage to say goodbye

When I first joined Mancini, there were some employees who had worked at the firm for years, but they weren't aligned with the firm's new direction. They weren't especially interested in doing bold work or pushing boundaries. They wanted to do the same job they'd been doing in the same way they'd been doing it for decades.

As I'm sure you can imagine, these employees weren't particularly excited when I showed up and told them, "I know you're a seasoned project accountant (for example), but you're going to do more than just billing. You're going to form relationships with clients and be a strategic partner to the project manager. You're going to get involved with the actual project, not just the billing." They simply weren't on board.

As leaders, we worked with them, we had tough conversations, we tried to get them on the same page. For months, even years, we kept those employees on staff. However, we eventually realized that we were doing both the firm and its employees a disservice.

As an organization, we weren't moving forward. We weren't progressing. We needed to make sure we had the right group of people to jumpstart the progress we wanted. Once we realized that stark fact, we made the bold decision to part ways with several employees.

During that time, I got some good advice. A mentor told me, "Envision where you want your group to go. Now, think about who is going to help you get there. Who do you need on your team?" Once I did that exercise, my decisions were clear.

As leaders, we had an honest reckoning and made tough decisions. Sometimes letting someone go results in a much better path for both that employee and all of the people they were working with. We didn't want to lose our best employees because they were tolerating coworkers who didn't want to be there, didn't pull their weight or didn't share the company's vision for the future. Once we had the right team, we were able to work in the right way on the right projects and move forward faster.

The courage to bet on big ideas

It takes courage to trust people, especially people who are big thinkers with bold new ideas. It's easy to stick with the status quo and stay where it's comfortable. It's easy to say no to new ideas, but to progress, in life and in our careers, we need to have an entrepreneurial spirit. We need the courage to say yes.

Before my current partners and I took over the firm, Mancini was traditional and old-school, mostly known for interior design projects. But after the financial crash in 2008, the firm needed to expand beyond one core sector if it wanted to last another 100 years. We started saying yes and leaning into our team's interests and passions.

THE POWER OF YES

Here's a couple of examples. A few years ago, an employee wanted to move the firm into the aviation sector, an industry we had never worked in before. We gave him the chance to do one small project in aviation. Fast forward a few years, and we're doing major aviation projects with a full and growing team and plenty of experience we can point to. If we as leaders had said no when that forward-thinking employee approached us, Mancini wouldn't be where it is now.

The same thing happened in technology. One employee had a big idea to push the firm into the twenty-first century using new tools like 3D printing and digital design. As a firm, we wanted to change the way we worked with clients and, more broadly, change the profession. That was a bold vision and we invested in it. We gave him the resources and space he needed to archetype his idea. We weren't sure what would unfold, but we were willing to see what happened.

He started with one 3D printer in a room, which he tested by making lampshades. Within a year, the 3D printing lab had expanded into a much larger operation. Now, we have a fleet of 3D printers and an entire Design Lab leading the way in the industry and we're known as a technology-first company, all based on saying yes to one visionary employee's idea.

Every time we have the courage to say yes to a big, scary, unproven idea, we accelerate our own growth and the growth of the person we say yes to, pushing forward together. Yes develops a rich set of experiences and projects that make us more attractive to team members and clients alike—and more likely to keep saying yes.

The courage to trust people

At Mancini, we've had the courage to say, "We're going to promote someone who is relatively inexperienced into a position with a lot of responsibility. We're going to give them the right tools, help them succeed and see how it unfolds." That decision has worked for us because we put a lot of trust in our people. We have the courage to trust that they will speak up if they need help, and our job as leaders is to help them flourish.

I have benefitted personally from this new trusting model of leadership. In an old-fashioned hierarchy, I'd probably still be in my former role as senior project accountant; I certainly wouldn't be CFO in my thirties. I might get there eventually, but not this quickly.

It's not about age, it's about appetite for opportunity. If someone is willing to step up and step into a role, whether they have experience or not, I'm willing to give them the chance. This decision to promote people based on their appetite for opportunity has been transformative for Mancini. It has pushed us forward as a company.

My challenge to you: find your courage. No matter where you are in your career—whether you're at the beginning, a moment of transition and change, or stepping into a leadership role—you'll need it.

BEING B.O.L.D.

Be yourself
Boldly, courageously be who you are.

Open your mind to new definitions and opportunities
Say yes! If you don't say yes, you'll never know what you could become. Say yes to your ideas and to the big ideas of the people around you. Keep your door and your mind open.

Lift others
Trust the people around you. It's courageous but beneficial to build a team, depend on others and help them flourish.

Don't wait—do it now
Take the first step. Getting started is often the hardest part.

5
Make New Rules

If you want to build something new, you'll probably need to do it in a new way. I realized early in my career that I would need to write my own playbook. I've never been someone who sticks to the status quo—I wanted to change things for the better.

When I joined Mancini as controller, I didn't have a clear picture of how to do my work, so I had to do a lot of reflection about what kind of leader I wanted to be. By the time I got promoted to CFO, I knew I didn't want to be the kind of leader who just sat in an office and issued occasional financial reports.

I had to ask myself, "How do I want to run my departments? How do I want to integrate my teams with the rest of the firm? How can I be a strategic partner with the CEO to run the firm effectively from both an operations and a financial standpoint? And what new rules can I write about how we'll all work together?"

My first decision as controller was that the rest of the leadership team needed to know exactly what was going on with the company financially. I started updating my partners every single week about the financial status of the organization—no matter the temperature, whether things were positive or going south, I wanted them to know. I didn't want them to be running blind. I wanted to make decisions jointly with the CEO, because every major decision he makes ties back to the finances.

To build a new way to run a firm, we need new rules. At Mancini, my partners and I have committed to rethinking old conventions. We're dedicated to doing business in a big, bold, radical way and putting our people first.

Here are a few ways those new rules for work have played out at our firm.

Leadership

The old rules: The most senior partners make the big decisions for the firm.

The new rules: Every employee group has a voice in the room where decisions are made.

First, we assembled a strong leadership team that bucked traditional definitions. Then, we thought about how we listened to the firm's employees. How could we make sure our decisions were informed by their good ideas, goals and aspirations? How could we connect employees to the firm's decisions and direction?

We decided to create a mixed leadership team that extends beyond the owners and principals, adding voices from the floor, including someone who is focused on technology and innovation, and a project manager who is in the thick of client work. We wanted to understand and hear from different people, and that change had an immediate impact.

Someone who works on the floor can speak up and advocate for their peers. They can say, "You're looking at this the wrong way." By bringing in new voices, we are utilizing the strength of the whole organization to help us make policies that work for everyone. Employees get a say in the highest-level conversations about how the firm is run. They know that their opinions and voices matter and we're collectively creating a firm we want to be a part of.

This gives new insights for us to reconsider how we as leaders nurture our people—including our promotion structure.

Promotions

The old rules: Promote people when they hit specific milestones.

The new rules: Promote people when they're ready.

Why should it take someone a long time to attain a particular title or responsibility? If someone is an associate, but they're proving themselves by doing the important work that a principal in the firm would do—like bringing in business, mentoring others, being a solid teammate—why make them wait for promotion? If they're showing they're ready to be a principal, why not promote them now?

The old way of thinking about a career progression works like this: someone applies for a role, gets the job and they do that role. They probably hope that by doing their work well, they'll get promoted. For some people, that path works, but it makes other people feel stagnant. They feel stuck on a wheel and lose connection to their work.

At Mancini, our goal is to create more connection and ignite people's enthusiasm. We ask how we can spark people into wanting to take charge of their careers. How do we help them see the fast growth they could achieve at our firm?

This desire to create a spark in our people and promote them faster meant we had to rethink another old-school practice: annual reviews.

Annual reviews

The old rules: Talk to your employees about their work and their career once a year. The employer is in charge of the career roadmap.

The new rules: Talk to your employees about their work and career on a regular basis. Each employee is in charge of their own career roadmap.

We call it the huMANCINI approach. Now, we as leaders work with our people to create a roadmap that reflects their interests, goals and what they want to see happen in their career. Then, we figure out how we can map their tasks and responsibilities along that path to make sure they can actually attain their goals in a realistic timeline.

Every person should be the CEO of their own career. They're in charge, and the question for their employer is, "How can we support this team member along their path? How do we nurture their talent and help them in reaching their goals?"

At Mancini, short monthly pulse reviews keep us in tune with employees and their career aspirations and dreams. Why would we wait for one day in the entire year to talk with them? The goal is to have a collective snapshot on a regular basis of how various topics are impacting our company growth and cultural integration.

Employees can also give feedback about how the firm is, or isn't, supporting them anonymously. We see this as a stepping stone toward helping them become comfortable with speaking openly about what they want and need.

So far, we've seen some of our top performers thrive under this new way of reviewing. People are rising to the occasion and raising their hands for new responsibilities. If someone comes to their manager and says, "I'm interested in nurturing our talent and want to be involved in the talent group," we give them that opportunity and include them in the process of interviewing and hiring employees. If someone has a passion for people, they shouldn't be limited to the responsibilities of the job they were hired for.

This mindset gives people new opportunities and helps them follow their interests and strengths. All they have to do is speak up, and we're ready to listen and respond.

Sharing the vision

The old rules: Give employees an annual update on the state of the company.

The new rules: Share frequently and transparently about the firm's status, progress and long-term vision.

Everyone at Mancini is CEO of their own career, but to build a strong firm, we also need to have a shared vision for where we're going together. We have to connect every employee to the long-term vision so that they can grow along with the firm.

Rethinking how to get people invested in our new ideas about how the firm would be run, we realized we'd need to have more frequent touchpoints with employees about what is happening. It would have been easy to put our heads down and focus on the day-to-day running of projects, losing sight of the big, shiny goals in the distance. We needed to keep everyone focused not just on today's work, but on tomorrow's possibilities. To do that, we needed to communicate frequently about those big goals.

Every third Thursday of the month, we have a town hall meeting with everyone in the firm. We update the team on new project wins, new project losses, the financial state of the company, promotions and any other news. It's a pulse of what's happening in the firm. Early on, we chose a few key metrics to represent how the firm is performing, and we update all employees about those metrics at every meeting.

But we've learned that those big firm-wide meetings aren't enough. Every manager and leader has to communicate the firm's vision to their team and make sure that every single employee feels connected to what's happening and where the firm is going. We learned this the hard way when we almost lost a key employee. He had attended all of our Thursday meetings, but he didn't see himself in the vision. He didn't see how his work contributed to where the firm was going.

My message to you: you could be rolling out the most exciting change you could ever have dreamed of, but if you aren't explaining it, if you're not showing people how they fit into your vision, they're not going to want to go along with you. They're not going to see themselves in your grand plan.

At Mancini, we have transformed the everyday connection between leaders and employees. We have created an approachable open-door culture. People know they can walk into a leader's office and have a conversation about anything. As leaders, we know that our job is to guide, direct, shape and nurture our people. We take that job very seriously.

Taking care of employees

The old rules: Culture leads to engagement and retention.

The new rules: Employees need more than culture. Make it easy for employees to commit to the organization by taking care of them through generous benefits.

Because I have a financial role, you might expect me to be fully committed to the bottom line. While it is, of course, important to me and I always want to run a profitable firm, I have a wider vision of success. For the leadership team at Mancini, our goal is not to end the year with a big pot of money for the owners. Instead, we want to think about and celebrate how we have supported our employees throughout the year to help them feel fulfilled and empowered.

One way we do that is through generous employee benefits. We give every employee a vacation stipend every year in addition to their paid time off. We want people to be able to go on vacation and unplug, and have a little bit of cash to help them do it. Taking time off to relax improves employees' well-being and helps them show up more fully at work. Sure, it costs the firm money to offer that stipend, but we know it's important. Our view is that we've all worked toward building this organization, so we should all benefit.

When employees see all the benefits you're giving them in addition to their salary, they'll likely want to do their best work and commit to the success of their projects and the firm. Profitability is essential, but it's not the only factor that matters. Give back to the people who have contributed to getting the firm where it is.

FINE-TUNE THE RULES AS YOU GO

As you're rewriting the rules for your own career or for an organization, it's important to stay flexible. One of the most critical lessons I carry with me is that changing the rules of work requires a lot of creativity and flexibility.

It might sound easy to make up a bunch of new rules. However, making changes takes time, and you can't decide how a firm will be run without working with the people who will be impacted. Experiment with changes. Some will work, some won't. When you realize that you're off track, find new ways to get everyone invested again. When you have new ideas, test them and fine-tune them. Ask people for their feedback. Always be exploring new ways to improve.

Remember, you aren't making rules in a vacuum.

At Mancini, many of our decisions and ideas are crowdsourced from employees in the firm. We lean on the strength of the people who work at the firm to help us create every policy. We have hired incredible talent and we know they have other skillsets they can bring to the table beyond the role they were hired to do. When we listen to our people, we help them push into their own potential.

I've learned that you always have to keep one eye on change. If you get too set in your ways, you'll just create a new set of old rules. Part of the magic of writing a new playbook and set of rules is staying open to more changes as you go. The new way of thinking is all about flexibility.

BEING B.O.L.D.

Be yourself
Every person should be the CEO of their own career, taking charge of their career roadmap rather than leaving the decisions to their employer.

Open your mind to new definitions and opportunities
Don't stick with the status quo—change things for the better. If you're not always flexible to change, you will merely create a new set of old rules.

Lift others
To have a seat at the management table in a company, an employee doesn't necessarily have to be one of the most senior at the firm. And promotions don't have to be based on milestones. It's far better to promote people when they're ready, regardless of their age.

Don't wait—do it now
Change the way you listen to employees / team members and make sure everyone is heard. It can have immediate positive impacts on your career and your company.

6
Transparency

It's great to be visible, but it's not enough just to show up. It's important to be visible *and* real.

Being fully transparent is what makes you relatable and authentic. People can see the real you and that helps build trust. They can only be motivated by your story if they can see themselves in it and envision themselves accomplishing something similar.

For all of my adult life, I have been transparent about my journey. One way I have shared it over the years is through social media. Early on, I decided that if I was going to put anything out on social media, it needed to be true to me. I wanted people to see themselves in my story. I wanted them to be able to take inspiration from it and apply it to their own journeys.

I think of my social media as a place to journal openly. I have an open Instagram account because I want people to be able to connect with me, and I want to have an impact on a larger scale than just my immediate circle. Over the years, my account has grown into a little community, and that's because I have been transparent. I've shared stories about my family, how I balance family life with my work and the different projects I've worked on.

I've always felt comfortable being open with people. I'm confident enough to "put myself out there" and vulnerable enough to talk about all the parts of my life. People see the successful part. They see the regular part. They see the mom. They see the CFO. People are drawn to me because they're able to relate.

SHARING THE GOOD, THE BAD AND THE UGLY

When I started using social media, there wasn't the pressure we see now to have perfect imagery. And maybe because I came to social media before the current age of perfection, I've always been OK sharing every side of myself, even the less "perfect" parts.

When I was pregnant with my son, I had a tough struggle with fibroids. I'd had fibroids prior to being pregnant, experienced fibroid degeneration during both of my pregnancies (the **worst** pain I could imagine), and a little over a year after my son's birth, I had surgery to take the fibroids out.

After my surgery, I detailed what had happened to me. The moment that I pressed "Post" on that story, I knew how vulnerable I was making myself, but I wanted to put myself out there. I immediately heard from so many people who had struggled with fibroids—women who had been experiencing difficulties getting pregnant because of them, or those who were trying to navigate decisions about surgery. My vulnerable story really resonated with those people. Just by writing out my experience, I connected with so many women.

When I became a leader, it was even more important for me to keep sharing. When I started doing things like going back to speak at school or at events, I felt like there was an onus on me to show people that success is attainable, whatever your circumstances, whoever you are. How could I show people that what I've achieved is attainable to them without actually putting myself out there and being transparent?

Seeing me achieve the role of CFO inspired people and gave them the confidence to reach for opportunities or apply for high-level positions they may not have considered before. I've heard from people who've said, "I saw you going for big things, and that was the push I needed. I'm glad I applied for the big job because I've learned so much about myself."

For me, getting that kind of feedback is wonderful. I don't want people to try to be like me; I want them to craft their own path and learn their own lessons along the way. Positive feedback confirms and validates what I'm doing, and makes me want to keep sharing.

Understand why you're sharing

There is one aspect of transparency that I've sometimes struggled with, and that's people who react negatively to what I share.

There are two ways people may react to my story. The first is taking it as inspiration, which is what I intend. But others feel overwhelmed or pressured. They say, "Who is this woman who has two kids, is a CFO and is doing a *lot* of things? How can I ever compare with that?" or "Just thinking about your life makes me tired." Over the years, when I've heard these reactions—when the comparisons come in—I've struggled with whether I should keep sharing.

I've had to get comfortable with knowing that I'm sharing **my** path and **my** journey. I shouldn't be shy about what I've accomplished. My job is to plant the seed of achievement in other people's minds. How that seed blooms and comes to life in the people who receive it isn't something I can, or want to, control, and I've had to make peace with that. The people who need that inspiration will take it. If people feel overwhelmed or compare themselves to me, that is their issue, not mine, so it shouldn't hold me back from sharing.

I don't share to tell the world about how many things I'm doing. It's not about that; it's about what's behind it. It's about the foundation. Whether people are working on one thing or ten different things, what I hope they take away from my story is the effort that I'm putting in. I want them to say, "I could apply that same effort and push into my own potential."

Before I share something on social media, I do a heart check to make sure I'm comfortable with the reasons why I'm sharing it. I come back to the core question: "Where is my heart?" My goal is not to be famous; I'm not seeking attention. I'm just a regular person who wants to show other regular people that big dreams are attainable and within reach. I hope they can apply the inspiration I intend to their own lives, journeys and careers. My goal is for other people, particularly women, to stop selling themselves short. That's why I'm comfortable being as transparent as I am.

Sharing your life and your career openly online may not be for you. There are costs to being transparent, but for me, the pros outweigh the cons. I've had to let go of what people may think about me or how they may respond and focus on the impact and the benefits they will get from seeing my playbook unfold in real time.

Transparency opens doors

What has my transparency done for my own journey? It has helped me grow my network exponentially. At this point, I am connected with a bunch of other women who have stories that are similar to mine or are leaders at their organizations. We're able to talk openly about the challenges and the successes that we're experiencing.

I've also seen my impact grow. Many of my nonprofit projects have been successful because I have shared them openly. It's not necessarily that my immediate contacts are not helping with the projects; it's that I share them widely and end up getting donations from people I don't even know. That's almost certainly because I reveal every step of what I'm building and doing. I share how the projects are unfolding. That open sharing builds trust, enhances my integrity and helps me build authentic relationships.

HOW OTHER PEOPLE'S TRANSPARENCY HAS HELPED ME

A lot of my peers have been transparent along their journeys, too, and I have learned from them. They have helped push me. I surround myself with high performers because I want to be pushed.

One of my girlfriends is what I call a "unicorn." Her star is rising fast. She started out as a pharmacist at a Rite Aid, and now she is the divisional vice president (VP) of pharmacy operations for the whole West Coast of the United States, managing hundreds of stores. She started at the bottom, she worked her way to the top, and she's not done. None of us is done. I draw huge inspiration from her story.

My best friend worked her way up within marketing in the nonprofit sector. She started as a production assistant and is now a director. I take inspiration from her story, too.

A lot of people don't choose to share their journeys publicly. A lot of people just want to do good work and keep their heads down. However, I think there needs to be more of us showing up and sharing our stories, more transparency.

THE IMPORTANCE OF TRANSPARENCY

Here's a story that showed me just how important it is to share and document our journeys, even when they're in progress. A friend googled "great architects." The names in the search results were all white men, most of whom were dead.

She reached out to Google and said, "There are so many women architects doing great things. Why aren't they shown?" A representative from Google replied with this:

"It's not up to us. These women don't show up in your search results because they're not documented. They aren't out there for our algorithm to find."

She started documenting her journey as a female architect, launching a movement called Beyond the Built to share the stories of minority architects who work in the built industry. Her goal is for these people's stories to show up at the top of page one of the Google results.

No matter what format you choose to share your journey, it is important to show up. There's strength in forming a community and showing up together. There's someone who needs to see you and learn from you being transparent.

The ripple effects of transparency

One big reason I share my story: I understand the power of the ripple effects.

For example, I have openly shared my work on my nonprofit, SheBuildsLives, from the beginning. As a result, I've had people reach out to me to tell me they have been inspired to start following their own dreams and goals.

They say things like, "I've always wanted to do something like this, but it seemed so huge. You showed me that I can start with just one project." If I'd kept that work private and never shared it publicly—if I'd decided to shield some part of myself—I never would have inspired those ripple effects.

Coincidentally, as I was writing this chapter, I got a message from a woman who said, "Thank you so much for sharing your story. I just completed my MBA because I was inspired by you. When you went back to school, I was encouraged to do the same." Like me, she has two kids and a full-time job. And she told me that whenever it got tough, she asked, "What would Bolanle do?"

She made it through! In her message, she told me that she'd just submitted her last paper. She'd finished her degree. Stories like that one show me transparency works. It has positive ripple effects.

Vulnerability

Writing this book is pushing me so much in terms of being vulnerable. You may think I'd be used to putting myself out there, but in these pages, I'm being transparent about all of the things that have gotten me to where I am—both the great times and the tough times. To a certain extent, I'm walking into the unknown, but I'm open to where this experience will lead me.

When I first considered writing a book, I had the idea that you couldn't document your life until you were at the end of a career. I had to drop that mindset and embrace the possibility of showing the playbook as it's unfolding. Why don't we talk to people about their journey until they're at the end? I want to be able to help people right now.

Transparency at work

I've had to learn how important it is to be transparent as an employee, and now as a leader at work. Every time I have been transparent, I've been able to grow and improve.

Transparency at work means being open about your strengths **and** your weaknesses. Then you can work with your leaders to help you improve, grow and get better at your role. Transparency allows the people around you to see and relate to the real you. If you're transparent about your weaknesses and show your team that you're determined to work through them, it can only work in your favor.

You can't move forward in the direction you want to go if you don't let other people know you and see you as you are.

It's OK not to be perfect

In our lives and workplaces, we have to be OK with being wrong. We have to be OK with making a mistake and being transparent about that. Embracing or working through our weaknesses doesn't take away from our strengths. When we're transparent about areas where we're lacking or that we're still working on, it doesn't detract from how powerful we are. It actually helps us improve.

Here's an example. I have always thought of writing as my weak point. In fact, I've always avoided it, but when I went back to school, my master's program required me to write all the time. I had to confront my weakness and fears around writing, so I went to a trusted girlfriend who is an excellent writer and shared my struggle and the vulnerability I was feeling. She worked with me, reviewed my writing and helped me build my confidence and improve.

Over the course of three years, I wrote all the words I'd been running away from for thirty years. I greatly improved in that area because I had been open, unafraid to name my weaknesses. I was OK with not being perfect.

My advice to you: drop the shield. Erase the facade. It's in moments of vulnerability when you can see huge growth. If you want to grow and move beyond your comfort zone, you'll have to be OK with feeling a little discomfort, embracing the unknown and being open about who you are, and vulnerable enough to share what you're going through.

At the same time, workplaces need to create cultures that allow for weakness. If you work in an environment where everyone puts up a perfect front, where no one can ever be wrong or the culture doesn't allow for weakness, you'll never feel comfortable showing up as your full self.

We made a conscious decision at Mancini to run a transparent firm. It's one thing to share the big-picture vision, but we also want to share information about how we're going to get to our targets and what kind of progress we're making.

That's why I feel passionate about openly sharing the firm's financials. When we have a town hall meeting and tell employees whether we're reaching or falling short of our goal, we're building trust with them. They have perspective on the decisions that are being made, which makes them feel included and motivated to contribute to our shared goals.

TOUGH DECISIONS IN 2020

We had to make tough decisions about the firm during the COVID-19 pandemic in 2020. It was a difficult year when we had to lay off or furlough some people, temporarily reducing salaries across the firm so that we could save jobs.

Every step of the way, we communicated those decisions with employees. We wanted to remove any room for misinterpretation. We told people, "The firm is going to run at a loss for the next six months. We need everyone to make a little sacrifice to get us past this and to make sure we all have jobs and can take care of our families." We had to be transparent about why we were making these decisions and when the issues would be resolved.

We're constantly updating and communicating so that the firm's employees trust us to lead them in the right direction.

I personally show up at work as an open book. I don't hide the fact that I have kids—and sometimes, when I don't have childcare, I bring them with me to work. In the thick of COVID, when everyone was at home (including kids!), I called in to a work meeting in which each team member reported on what we had done that day. Being truly transparent, I was honest.

"I couldn't really work. I had two toddlers I had to fully focus on and I could only offer 10% today." It was important for me to be open. As the CFO, if I can't be honest when things are less than perfect for me, how can I expect any other employee to be honest about what they can handle and contribute?

When I vocalize my struggles, I set an example and allow other people to be realistic about their struggles. I can't pretend like all of the balls are in the air and everything's going smoothly.

Here's my challenge to you: be more transparent in every part of your life.

BEING B.O.L.D.

Be yourself
Don't hide your struggles. Resist the urge to put up a facade. Let people in.

Open your mind to new definitions and opportunities
It might seem counterintuitive, but sharing your authentic self (including your weaknesses) can open doors and allow you to learn and grow in new ways. Lean into it.

Lift others
Set the example, and then take other people as they are, too. Remember that everyone has their own struggles and challenges.

Don't wait—do it now
If you have been afraid to share your authentic story, start practicing now. How could you be more transparent at work, with your family, in your friendship group or online? Practice sharing openly and you'll get more comfortable over time.

7
Be Generous

Giving is my love language. I think of generosity as the most important character trait. Giving your resources, time or money to improve people's lives and help them—what more is there to life than that?

At my core, generosity is who I am, and I truly believe that it has been key to getting me where I am today. Giving back is my natural disposition. Even if generosity doesn't come naturally to you, it is something you can practice and build over time.

When you give, it's not about you—it's about the person who is receiving. You remove the focus from yourself. I've seen how that can lead to change, growth and real magic. Generosity has certainly created magic in many different parts of my life.

Giving back

I've talked about my hobby of crocheting hats. I've talked about my nonprofit that helps kids in Nigeria, and I've talked about my own children and my family. But I haven't told you the story of how all of those things fit together.

SheBuildsLives was born out of loss. A decade ago, my husband and I were trying to have a baby. I had fibroids, which often impact fertility, but my doctors encouraged me to go ahead. After a year, I was finally pregnant in December of 2012. However, a few weeks later, around Christmas, I had a miscarriage.

I was devastated. To get my mind off the pain of the miscarriage, I started crocheting. Knitting and crocheting are skills I picked up from my late grand aunt when I was younger. I've always been fascinated by using my hands in this way, taking little steps one at a time to create a masterpiece. At that moment, crocheting became a therapeutic outlet for me. It allowed me to re-center my mind, taking it off of the loss I had just experienced and focusing it instead on making something beautiful for others.

At first, I made hats for my godchildren and my friends' kids, but then, I decided that I should be giving the hats to babies in the neonatal intensive care unit (NICU). One of my friends was working at an NICU, so I started with a small project—crocheting thirty hats for her hospital. I called it BolaKraft Cares, and I dropped off that donation on May 1.

The next day, on May 2, I found out I was pregnant again, with my daughter. It felt completely serendipitous. I had found an avenue to help other children and stop focusing on myself, and at the same moment, God had blessed me with my own child.

That's how SheBuildsLives was born. I knew I had to keep giving back to kids who needed a little extra help, and I saw how living with a spirit of generosity gave me a fulfilled life. That experience explains why I continue to carry so much passion for SheBuilds-Lives—it is directly connected to my daughter. It's her legacy as much as it's mine.

Expanding my impact

I have always had a passion for education, but having my own children made me even more passionate about providing all children with access to learning, resources and the feeling that someone out there cares about their future. For me, it made sense that I would explore projects for children back home in Nigeria.

When I looked at kids in Nigeria who didn't have the environment or the education to become whatever they wanted to be, their situation felt unfair. I saw a worldwide issue of inequality and a lack of resources, and I wanted to make my own small contribution to helping those children wherever and however I could.

Looking for a project in Nigeria, I talked to a friend who was doing work in Makoko, Lagos, a water community where everyone lives in houses built on stilts. My friend was trying to raise money for desks in the community school. Maybe I could knit scarves, sell them and use the funds to buy these desks.

I posted about the project on Instagram and the response was incredible. People wanted to help. And a lot of people didn't even care about getting a scarf—they just wanted to donate to the cause because it was meaningful. That was my first school project in Nigeria, and from there I kept going.

Next, I wanted to do a project in Borno, the region where the terrorist group Boko Haram had kidnapped hundreds of girls from their school. My cousin happened to be friends with a reporter who was traveling in Borno, in the town of Chibok. He shared how education had stopped in the region after the kidnapping because it wasn't safe to send kids to school. The reporter told me that new schools had just opened, and they needed funds.

Through social media and word of mouth, I told the story of these children who had been out of school for years, and how SheBuildsLives could help them get back. I raised over $4,000 to support 500 students attending a school in Chibok.

Next, I did a project in the state where I'm from, Delta, to raise $4,000 to build bathrooms and buy textbooks for a primary school. As I worked on these projects, I realized that I was enjoying the impact I was making, but I wanted to learn more. That's when I decided to get my degree in education and social policy.

During this time, I was moving up in my career and I had less opportunity to use my hands on my crocheting projects. I would crochet on the train to and from school, but I didn't have time to make as much as I had been, so I started thinking about the bigger picture. How could I focus SheBuildsLives on bigger projects in the education space? How could I make more of an impact?

In 2019, SheBuildsLives achieved its biggest project yet: building an elementary school in Makoko, Lagos.

That was my first fundraiser over $20,000 and I was proud of creating such a major impact.

My goal with SheBuildsLives is to build schools and learning centers that are safe spaces for the children of Nigeria. But I'm also thinking about what other pain points these communities are facing. Lack of education is not their only problem; people are also wondering how they're going to feed their families, so if a learning center can provide a free breakfast or lunch, that's one thing off parents' shoulders. Kids in Nigeria need healthcare, so SheBuildsLives is finding ways to provide it through the schools. And when COVID hit, kids couldn't go to school, so SheBuildsLives needed to find ways to reach them. The government was broadcasting school lessons, but many people didn't have TVs, so SheBuildsLives provided radios.

Essentially, SheBuildsLives wants to know what the things are that affect a child. How can we either partner with other organizations or build an ecosystem to address those issues?

In 2021, I got a big opportunity to make a policy-level impact for one state in Nigeria. A friend, working with the state to plan an education summit, asked, "What is the current state of education in the area? How can we have conversations about what we need to do to improve?" I came on board as a technical consultant, drawing on my educational policy degree to ask the right questions and move the conversation in the right direction. The primary stakeholder in all of these discussions should be the children (not teachers or politicians).

When I reflect back on my journey and the impact I've made over the past eight years, I feel amazed. It all started with one decision to crochet thirty hats, that one small project leading to bigger projects impacting more and more kids. I have always started small, one project at a time.

I'm passionate and excited about what SheBuilds-Lives can do. It's something I will always find time for. I do this work because it impacts lives. It impacts the next generation, and it impacts me. It is fulfilling to do something that's not just about myself or my family, but builds other people up.

R.E.A.C.H. NIGERIA

Beyond being generous with my own time and resources, I'm looking for ways to encourage other people to be generous. A few years ago, I was having conversations with Nigerians living in the U.S. who wanted to do something back home, but they didn't know where to begin or who to talk to. That's when I started an organization called R.E.A.C.H. (Responsible Engagement through Awareness and Community Help) Nigeria.

R.E.A.C.H. Nigeria connects people with causes and organizations where they can give back. So many people want to show their generosity, so R.E.A.C.H. Nigeria is a connector hub that puts them in touch with work they're interested in. It amplifies volunteer opportunities and spotlights nonprofits that are on the ground so that people can support their mission and be a part of their work.

Building this hub has been an eye-opener, because I've found so many people who are truly passionate about giving back. There's so much good being done, we just need more people to help. If R.E.A.C.H. Nigeria is able to amplify the work people are doing on the ground, it can increase their impact.

Generosity at work

It's important to help others in your work life. Leadership is not about making it to your seat at the table, and then doing your own thing; you have to give back so that your organization can move to where you need it to go. A generous leader is always a better leader.

One trope I'd like us to rethink is the "career ladder." I don't just want to get to the top of my own ladder; I want to help other people build and climb up their ladders, too. Now that I'm at a higher rung, I think about how I can make it a little easier for the people coming up behind me. How can I help them move up faster?

My understanding about how to move up at work has completely changed. It's not about heads-down work; it's about making ourselves visible. I now use my voice to speak up about other people's good work and make **them** visible.

As a leader, I have the chance to set new rules and write a new playbook for how an organization should be run. All leaders can create a better, more sustainable, more fulfilling work environment for everyone. Generous leaders don't just keep enforcing the old rules because they've always been there. They think differently about what new rules and actions will create success.

Mentorship

This brings us to why mentorship is so important to me. I'm the first black CFO many people have ever met. I'm proud of that, and I'm proud that I've got over the hurdle of being the "first," but I don't want to be the "only." I want to see more people like me in roles like mine, to make sure there are more people coming up behind me.

I don't believe in protecting my gains or keeping my progress for myself. There's no joy in that. My organization and my industry will be stronger with more diverse points of view from diverse leadership.

Mentors give you an outside opinion from someone who believes in you, is reaching for your success and can provide insight, support and guidance while you're navigating career decisions, big or little. Mentors bring flavor to a career. My mentors have had a powerful impact on my success, and now as a leader and a mentor to others, I've seen the positive change I can bring about by sharing my time, money, resources and knowledge. It's extremely fulfilling to share information with someone who is coming up in their career and see the scales fall from their eyes when they realize what they can accomplish because of my help. Generosity can create mindset shifts in others. I've seen it happen.

I first started mentoring young people through my church, and over the years I have mentored a lot of people who needed guidance in their careers. Right now, I am mentoring two young women who are in year one of starting their business. Sometimes the things I say to them sound simple to me, but to them, the advice is a game-changer. They can learn from me so they don't repeat the mistakes that I made in their business.

If we want the next crop of employees to be great, we have to carve out the time to guide them. Mentorship is a good way to be generous with our time and pass along what we have learned, making the path a little easier for the people coming behind us.

Another key way leaders can give back is through serving on boards of organizations they're passionate about. If launching your own nonprofit project on the side isn't realistic, you could donate your time to a board that could use your experience, expertise and professional connections. I encourage all leaders to give back in this way.

Go and give

I have seen how generosity *unlocks* possibilities for other people, and for the giver. It unlocks people's full potential. When you act from a place of generosity, you move through life as a happier, healthier person. Being generous can only improve your wellbeing. There's a sense of fulfillment that comes from doing things for others and loving on them. Giving has certainly challenged me and pushed me to grow.

Generosity for me might look like taking on mentees, speaking at events and sharing my story, or creating SheBuildsWaves and SheBuildsMoney. The common thread is that all of my projects are "purpose to impact." In other words, I know the purpose behind them, and that purpose is to have a positive impact on people's lives by finding ways to be generous.

Everyone has a role to play in helping others. I offer you a simple question: how can you act on your purpose and make an impact on others? Your answer doesn't have to be big or complicated. It could be one small step toward helping someone else; the important thing is to just get started. Start giving and you'll keep pushing yourself into your full potential and others into theirs.

BEING B.O.L.D.

Be yourself
Generosity unlocks your full potential and expands your impact.

Open your mind to new definitions and opportunities
Look around your community or around the world. What opportunities are there to make people's lives better? What opportunities can you see to help eradicate inequality?

Lift others
When you give, it's not about you—it's about the person who is receiving. I've seen how that can lead to change, growth and magic. It is fulfilling to do something that's not just about you, but builds other people up.

Don't wait—do it now
There will always be people out there who need your help right now. Go find them, right now!

8

Build Community

A big theme in my career has been the power of community. It's important to ask yourself these three questions at every step of your career:

1. How am I building community around myself?

2. How am I building community in my organization so that we can retain people and create a sense of belonging?

3. How am I fostering connections beyond my organization?

Let's think about community at those three different levels.

Building a community as you build your career

Early in my career, I didn't think much about intentionally finding a community. With the financial crisis swirling around me, I was just trying to make sure I had a job! I didn't explore professional communities for years. Instead, my community came from personal connections.

I needed people around me to give confirmation and affirmation to my desires and dreams to move up in my career, so I went on to create a business community for myself. The people closest to me were my sounding boards, my cheerleaders, the ones who helped me mastermind career moves and side projects.

When I became CFO and part owner of Mancini, it was important for me to find a more formal network of women in similar roles, making high-level decisions. Over the years, I've found that community of high-performing women who are "going for it." This personal community of peers has helped me navigate my path and propel me to where I am now.

I didn't understand the value of a more formal community until my mid-career. Looking back, I realize that I could have found more support if I had plugged into a community much earlier. Even once I had risen to the top of my organization, I still needed a community. We all do.

A friend told me about Chief, a private network for C-suite and VP-level women. I applied, and I'm now part of a group of ten women who work with each other and an executive coach. Even though we work in different industries, we all help each other and offer each other a diversity of opinions. I can ask a question and get help from the community to solve it.

I can grow and move faster and more easily when I'm part of a collective. Chief has helped me learn new things I wouldn't have explored on my own.

TEN WOMEN TO WATCH

Looking for inspiration? These women are creating new definitions, pushing into their potential and lifting others as they climb:

- **Pascale Sablan,** associate, Adjaye Associates and founder and executive director, Beyond the Built Environment. I'm inspired by Pascale's dedication to advocacy. She is the 315th living registered African-American female architect in the United States, and she is working to change the face of architecture.

- **Julia Gamolina,** director of strategy, Trahan Architects and founder and editor in chief, *Madame Architect*. I'm inspired by Julia's commitment to making extraordinary women in the profession visible through her online publication, *Madame Architect*.

- **Omonye Phillips,** divisional VP, Rite Aid Pharmacy and co-founder, My Dream BIG Club. Omonye's career journey inspires me. She started as a pharmacist and worked her way up to divisional VP overseeing 200+ stores. That is phenomenal, and she's still rising—and lifting others. My Dream BIG Club helps entrepreneurs jumpstart their businesses.

- **Meaghan Murphy,** editor in chief, *Woman's Day*. Meghan is high-energy and always spreading positivity. She inspires me by how authentically she lives her life—she's built her career boldly while having a great time with her family. Check out her book, *Your Fully Charged Life*.[1]

- **Samantha Josaphat-Medina,** founder and principal, Studio 397. Samantha is the 397th licensed African-American female architect in the U.S, an accomplishment she proudly displays in her firm's name. She's a trailblazer who keeps making room to lift other female architects. She has served as the president of the New York Chapter of the National Organization of Minority Architects, which champions diversity within the design profession.

- **Osayi Alile,** CEO, Aspire Coronation Trust Foundation. Osayi was one of my early career role models. I have known her since I was eleven years old, and her leadership journey gave me a model to work toward. Her organization funds nonprofits in

---

1   M.B. Murphy *Your Fully Charged Life: A radically simple approach to having endless energy and filling every day with YAY* (Tarcherperigee, 2021)

Nigeria. She is also former chairperson of the board of Women in Management, Business and Public Service (WIMBIZ), a group dedicated to elevating women.

- **Julie Hiromoto,** principal and director of integration at HKS. Julie is a former colleague and I have huge respect for her expertise at delivering large-scale projects, including One World Trade Center. She received the American Institute of Architects' (A.I.A.) 2019 Young Architect Award, has taught sustainability courses at NYU, is an ambassador for the International Living Future Institute and a mentor for the next generation of architects.

- **Adeola Whitney,** CEO, Reading Partners. Adeola is an experienced leader who is dedicated to lifting others up. She has been like a big sister to me, listening to my ideas, pointing me in the right direction and giving me a model for strong and supportive female leadership.

- **Yiselle Santos,** VP and director of justice, equity, diversity and inclusion (J.E.D.I.), HKS. Yiselle is an advocate for J.E.D.I. at work—and is working toward the day when firms don't need J.E.D.I. experts anymore. She serves on the A.I.A. national board and is founder of Women Inspiring Emerging Leaders in Design (W.I.E.L.D.).

- **Cyndie Spiegel,** founder and president of Dear Grown Ass Women. Cyndie inspires women to show up as themselves, act boldly and move past society's expectations. She is building boldly herself, and her honesty and authenticity inspire me.

Build a community at your organization

As a leader, creating community within your workplace is incredibly important. If you want to retain great employees, they need to feel included. People need to feel like they belong to something bigger than themselves, connecting with the mission of the organization. How do you get a diverse group of people to pull in the same direction, toward shared goals? The answer is community.

The way I've always built these all-important work communities is through communication. We've talked about the power of transparency at work. At Mancini, we value communicating openly and being real with employees every step of the way. That makes them feel like they're part of the Mancini community. It makes them more productive and more motivated to do good work. They feel like they belong.

When employees don't feel like they belong, they start to feel stagnant instead. They aren't anchored to what the organization wants to accomplish, so can't move together as one.

When leaders create communities among their teams and in their organizations, everything improves. When you draw people in, include them in the mission and ask for their feedback, you create a more cohesive unit. The end product will be better, teams will be more successful, and people will feel like their voices are being heard and their contributions are part of something bigger. They'll feel like they can show up as themselves in a safe community.

During COVID, the importance of community became much more obvious to me. A lot of mothers, in particular, were pushed out of the workforce because they had to make choices between caring for their families or doing their work. I would never want to create an environment where a mom had to make that choice. I want to create a community where working moms feel like they belong—a community that promotes flexibility and values parents.

This isn't just something to do to be nice. In my experience, you won't find a more efficient worker than a working mom. She doesn't have enough time to be anything but efficient, so we can all benefit from building a workplace that is inclusive of mothers.

But it's not just mothers—we need work communities that include everyone: people with disabilities; people with different identities; people who have other responsibilities outside of work. I want to create a space that honors everyone and allows them to show up as they are and do their best work. They need to feel like there's space for them to contribute, speak up and be heard, and make the changes they'd like to see within the organization. I want people to bring their hard skills, their human skills and their ideas to work. I want to give people space to do what they're really good at and flourish.

At Mancini, we pay attention to everything that makes each person special, and that attention makes employees feel happy and fulfilled. Once people feel truly valued, the bottom line automatically comes through. At Mancini, we've seen it happen.

Even though I'm a numbers person, my focus as a leader is always on people. People are the ones doing the work. Once they know the firm is invested in them, they'll use that support to do their best work. My partners and I have created the type of firm we would have loved to work in when we were coming up. We've created the type of firm we want to work in now and that will help us attract the people we need to continue to succeed.

Often, people don't like to use the words "care" or "empathy" at work. When I have felt cared for, I have been able to do my best work, so as a leader, I will always create a space where other people feel cared for. Community, at its heart, is about taking care of each other.

If you're a leader and you feel skeptical about this message, if you feel like this perspective is too idealistic, I challenge you to try it. These are big shifts, so you likely won't see big changes happen overnight. You have to be patient, but when you stop thinking about people transactionally, when you start showing people you care, you'll see a change happen.

Foster new connections

I'm very focused on building a community beyond my own personal sphere or work. When I think back on my career journey, I see that I mostly found my way on my own, and certainly without the support of professional organizations. Sure, I had peers who guided me and helped me figure things out along the way, and I managed to create a path in finance within the architecture industry, but something was missing. I hadn't necessarily found "my people."

There are others like me out there—other accountants who are moving up in the industry. When I was starting out, people who work in architecture, but in the behind-the-scenes functions (finance, legal, HR) didn't have a professional organization to show them what was possible in their careers. They were, and often still are operating in isolation and trying to figure things out on their own. Even though their work is integral to the success of client projects, they are often overlooked in their organizations since they're not the face of the work, they aren't delivering to clients.

Plus, in functions like accounting, there's limited career progression. Once you make it to senior accountant, you might be able to move to a different firm, but there likely won't be a clear way to make sure you grow in your role in your current organization. For these reasons, the people who work in architecture's support roles often end up getting stuck. They stay in one role for decades.

That's not what I wanted for myself, so I wondered how I could create an organization where people like me, who have made a home in the architecture industry, could come together and have conversations, not just about developing hard skills, but about how we show up in our careers and beyond. That's what I was thinking about when I started SheBuildsWaves. I wanted to create a community where women would feel a sense of belonging.

SheBuildsWaves brings together a collective of women across different departments within the architecture industry to talk about challenges they face along their career paths and share strategies to find fulfillment at work. I want them to see that the industry cares about them. I want to show them that their work matters and is critical to their organizations' success.

The first event SheBuildsWaves hosted was called Quarterly Conversations. We pulled in panelists from all levels of their careers to share their real, honest experiences. They weren't saying they had it all figured out, or that there's one right way to build your career; they were just holding space so people could see the real, unique paths others had taken and learn from each other about how to navigate their own paths. Later, SheBuildsWaves started a series called Growth Workshops to help anyone in the industry, regardless of department or title, get the skills and tools they need to grow.

That first event welcomed twenty to thirty women, the next one grew to fifty. People started feeling like they had a space where they could talk openly about the good and the bad, things that were bothering them and their wins and successes. They were keying into each other's stories, leaving events feeling bolstered, confident and inspired. They no longer felt dormant or stuck or like they were just coasting along; they had an action plan. They saw people like them who were achieving things, and they got the motivation they needed to push into their potential, grow and make changes in their careers.

People also realized they wanted to be a part of the community. Women who were twenty years into their careers reached out to me and said, "I wish something like this had existed when I first started out. I felt so lonely. I didn't know how to handle certain conversations at work, but if I'd had a community like this, I would have had a space to discuss these things. I would have had relationships outside of my own organization." I felt a responsibility to bring those people together and foster those connections. I wanted to give them a place and a voice in their industry.

Starting this group has made me realize the power of seeing ourselves in other people. We are all learning and there are people out there who can help us navigate or avoid the hard things they went through. We don't need to sweat or suffer. If we engage with people who have already navigated their path and are willing to share their stories transparently in a community, they can help us figure things out.

No matter where you are in your career, you can join an organization or a community (or create your own) to connect with others, start conversations, feel a sense of belonging and understand that you aren't the only one going through your particular challenges. I continue to work to bridge the gap between architects, designers and the "behind-the-scenes" employees in other departments, and one of my major goals with SheBuildsWaves is to foster more inclusivity within the built industry. Our mission is to break down barriers, help women take charge of their careers and motivate them to push into their potential. At some point, we'd like to help even more women beyond this industry. We want to keep making bigger waves.

We can all build stronger communities in every part of our lives by remembering the B.O.L.D. framework.

BEING B.O.L.D.

Be yourself

To build community with others, you have to let them in. Show up as you are, transparently and generously. When you go first, you'll encourage others to show up as their full authentic selves, too.

Open your mind to new definitions and opportunities

How could you build a community where it doesn't exist already? How could you bring people together cross-functionally, across industries or across traditional boundaries? What communities do you wish you'd had when you were younger, and how could you build them now?

Lift others

We all achieve more when we create space and connections for others. If you had a powerful mentor or community early in your working life, how could you recreate that nurturing experience for someone else now? If you didn't have the support you needed, how could you change that story for the next generation? How could you practice community by taking care of others?

Don't wait—do it now

You're never too young or too inexperienced to start connecting people. You don't have to wait until you're experienced or well-connected "enough." Reach out and form connections, community and collectives right now. The sooner you start building a community, the faster you'll be able to push into your potential.

9
Your Legacy Starts Now

"Legacy" is a word that people usually think about at the *end* of their career, but we're all making small changes and taking strides forward every day. All of those moments add up over time to create our legacy. That's why I think about "legacy" as something that's happening now. In the present.

We can all ask ourselves, "What are the things I'm doing right now (as a leader or as an employee) to build my legacy?" Legacy is not one stagnant experience—it's made up of everything we've done until now and everything we're still working on. For me, legacy is my foundation, my values, my vision and how I'm impacting the people around and beyond me.

Legacy starts early

The characteristics of a leader don't just show up the day you're promoted. Leadership is a muscle you strengthen over time, and the earlier you start building it, the better.

My actions as an employee, even early in my career, afforded me the ability to become a leader. In my early days of working, I had a mindset that I needed to do more than just take care of myself. I wanted to build something bigger for other people, too. That mindset and vision helped me get where I am today. It separated me from the pack.

Looking back, I wasn't intentionally building a legacy in my early days; I was just trying to get my foot in the door! But when I got the call about the opportunity at Mancini, I realized that I had spent ten years building my early career legacy through every interaction I'd had with people at work. It was built through nurturing relationships, finding solutions, volunteering for more responsibilities, helping my firm get through the financial crisis, and always making sure I was showing up and showing value. At every inflection point in my career, I found my voice a little more. I discovered more courage, communicated the value I was bringing better and nurtured my relationships more. I built a pattern of being bold.

Many of my bold actions in my early career were about *influence*. When I was a project accountant, I broke the status quo by making myself visible to the teams on the floor, talking to them regularly about their project status and asking to come to project sites. My behavior changed the way people thought about their accounting groups. I influenced other accountants to work differently, deepen their relationships with the project teams they supported and broaden their impact.

Even though I can't claim that I was focused on "building a legacy" early on, I did think about what people would say about me if I left the firm. What would they remember about my time there? I never wanted to leave an organization and wonder if people were glad I had gone. I wanted people to remember that I'd watched out for them, not just myself. I wanted them to remember their experiences with me in a positive light.

Vision and values

Most of the time, we're acting out our values without realizing it or thinking about it. Our decisions and actions come naturally when they're aligned with our values, but we all have to make an intentional decision.

We have to ask ourselves, "What are my values? What are the principles I want to be known for? What guides me?"

Don't wait until you're starting a C-level job to ask these questions and set your values. It starts early. One part of pushing toward big goals is developing your own awareness of what you want to see happen and the value system you need to put into place to achieve that vision.

HOW TO DEFINE YOUR VISION

Have you ever made a vision board? Let's make one now. No matter where you are in your career, you can take a few minutes to clarify and define your vision and start working toward a legacy.

- **What are three things you want people to say about you?** What are the values you want to model through your actions? *Example: "I lift other people up."*
- **Write down your top three goals.** What do you want to accomplish over the course of your career? Name what you want to see happen. *Example: "Improve ethnic diversity at my organization by 20%."*
- **Reflect on where you are.** What are you doing and accomplishing right now?
- **Define the gap between where you are now and what you want to accomplish.** What stands between you and where you want to go?
- **Plan small steps to work toward your goal.** What is one action you could take now? Keep in mind

that you will need to be flexible on your journey to accomplish your goals. If you want to get from 0 to 100, first think about how you could get from 0 to 10, and then 10 to 20. How can you take small steps each day to get closer to your vision?

- Do your **goals** align with your **values**? How could you move toward your goals **while** living out your values?

Take steps toward your dreams

Throughout the book, I've shared with you some of the many projects that I'm juggling—my professional role and my nonprofits—but there's one other project I haven't mentioned.

Recently, my husband and I created a business for our children: an event rental company for party supplies like bounce houses. Rental companies are profitable, so we created it as an income stream that will go to our children. We're thinking ahead for them, wanting a better life for them.

One of my strengths is not just thinking about something, but actually pulling out the inspiration, motivation, energy and will to execute it. Sometimes, I share on Instagram about the company and my kids' role in it, and when I share these things, people can be overwhelmed at the work it must take.

"How do you do all of this?" is a question I often hear. My goal isn't to overwhelm anyone with what I'm doing now. What they don't see is the years of work and thought that went into each project to lay the groundwork for them.

My goal in sharing projects like this publicly is to nudge people into changing their mindset. My capacity to follow my dreams might be higher than average, or the structure of my life might be different than other people's, but I want my story to influence them to ask themselves, "What is **one thing** that I want to do? How can I plant the seeds now so that one day, I will look back and realize I've accomplished my dreams through slow, steady action?"

My legacy is about changing mindsets. I want people to think bigger and build boldly—to take action. One of my goals is to inspire others to move and act on ideas or impulses that have been dormant in them.

Changing people's mindsets was one of my goals when I started R.E.A.C.H. Nigeria. I wanted to get more people thinking about helping others. If I could show them causes that would tug at their hearts, they'd be likely to ask, "How can I help?"

At this point in my career, I realize I'm talking from a place of privilege. Leadership has afforded me more flexibility in my schedule, so I can prioritize time differently than I could when I was an entry-level employee.

However, even if you're working a nine-to-five and you don't have much flexibility, I encourage you to find small moments when you can work toward your goals. When I was in my twenties, I was knitting hats on my commute. There's always opportunity for you to work toward building your legacy, no matter what phase of life you're in.

I think of myself as a serial solution seeker: I'm always asking myself how I could provide a solution. When people see the solutions I'm creating, I hope that they're inspired to look within themselves and ask, "What solution is within me?" What about you? What change could you make in your workplace, as an entrepreneur or in your community? What work could you do that ties back to your values? What actions could you put into motion to produce a positive outcome?

The idea of a living long-term legacy is important. People tend to think legacy happens when you're thirty years into your career, but every single thing you do, every single experience, every single contact you make ties into what your overall legacy will be.

Achieving your goals

When thinking about achieving their goals, people often look for an easy way to "make it" or speed up their progress. Take it from me: there is no easy way. No shortcut. No magic trick or "hack."

When people ask me, "How do you do it all?", I know they expect to hear about some secret silver bullet. But instead, I give them a simple answer: "I get $%!& done!" I am disciplined and consistent; I know what I want to happen, and I know I have to be disciplined about working toward it. Sure, you can follow the mantra of "working smarter, not harder." For me, that means knowing what I want to accomplish and how to best use my energy to get there.

This is what works for me:

1. Work in harmony with your energy patterns.

2. Take small steps.

3. Put support systems in place.

4. Slow down to speed up.

Work in harmony with your energy patterns

A lot of people work against themselves because they don't take advantage of the times of day they're most productive. Between 5 and 8 a.m. is my most productive time.

This awareness was my first step toward realizing my goals. Then I had to change my schedule to act on that awareness. Now I wake up early because I know that's when I perform the best. I maximize that time.

Take small steps

I'm a big fan of setting specific, measurable, achievable, relevant and time-bound (S.M.A.R.T.) goals. I break my big goals down into steps I can measure so that I can reflect periodically on my progress. In other words, instead of trying to go from 0 to 100, first I go from 0 to 10. Then I think about the next step.

In my experience, small actions lead to change starting to happen. Take control of your time and the things you can change, working in little increments.

Put support systems in place

Once I've identified my energy patterns and determined the steps to take, my next recipe for success is making sure I have the right support systems in place. That is how I win and stay consistent more days than not.

In my home, at work, in my organizations, I have set up systems to make sure tasks are accomplished. For example, one of the ways I win with consistently exercising is having my workouts already created, so that when I get in the gym, there is no room for guessing. I just get to work.

Slow down to speed up

This is one of my favorite mantras. Often, we set a goal, and then start running towards it, but I've seen how important it is to pause, check in and understand what's working and what's not.

Do a monthly check-in with yourself. Are you still on track to where you want to go? If not, what's slowing you down or sending you off course?

When you slow down to speed up, it might seem like everyone else keeps running past you. Don't worry about them. When you slow down, you can fine-tune your process and fix what isn't working. Then, when you start running too, you'll be able to go faster than everyone else for longer, and more consistently.

Many times in my work, I've seen the value in slowing down to speed up. The COVID-19 pandemic was a natural slow-down time for many people around the world, and it definitely was for me. I used it to regulate my energy and my journey. Before the pandemic, I was always on the go, speaking at events, traveling. I was building up to making a big impact. When COVID happened, it was tough to have to slow down and take stock of everything I was doing. For people like me who are highly creative, always thinking, stretching and strategizing, there was certainly a fear of losing momentum. When I reflect on this time,

I realize that I'd been given a gift. I had time to take a look at all of the balls I had in the air, all of the things I was doing, and fine-tune them.

A pandemic is a drastic reason to slow down. We can all build in small slow-down moments throughout the year. These are chances to honor our season of life, make sure we're not running at full speed for too long and reduce the risk of burning out.

What do I mean by seasons of life? At the moment, I am in a planting season. I'm planting many seeds in my life, and this planning and building phase often needs to be slow and painstaking. Other people can't necessarily see the work I'm doing because I'm just laying the groundwork behind the scenes. I'm making sure my foundation is strong. I'm putting the right support systems in place around me, and I'm motivated because I have an exciting harvest season to look forward to. I'm preparing myself now for the speed-up time that is around the corner.

Because I know what season I'm in and I respect this moment, I don't let myself get distracted by other people who are in a different season. When you're planting, don't worry about the people who are harvesting. Don't compare yourself. They probably spent years in their own planting season. Support them and cheer them on, knowing you'll be in that season at some point, too.

Hopefully you can learn from my working habits, but remember there is no magic hack. In terms of actually moving toward your goals, it's all about consistently working on the small steps every single day.

My vision for the future

As I close this chapter, I'm thinking about the legacy I want to continue to build. What's next?

My vision for Mancini Duffy

At Mancini, I want to make sure my work leads to financial success for the firm and everyone who works there. We're in an exciting time of growth and innovation, making huge leaps in how we use technology. What's next is making a broader impact on the profession. We want to change the way people in the built industry work.

Now, clients come to us specifically because of our tech-centered process. Mancini is building a legacy of using technology to challenge our clients and peers to think differently about how they work. I'm excited for the ride. I don't know exactly where it's taking us, but I'm excited to see what we come up with.

One of my other priorities is representation, diversity and inclusion, both at Mancini and more broadly in the built industry. Like my friend Yiselle Santos, I want to see a time when organizations don't have to hire J.E.D.I. experts to start these conversations. What can I do in my work as a leader so that my organization doesn't need someone in that role? How can we build a more inclusive, diverse, equitable firm and apply those changes across our industry?

It's my responsibility as one of the people currently in leadership positions to be a part of making that change. It's easy to assume that it's someone else's job to make big changes—as if there's some secret society somewhere making all of the rules. But no. It's on all of us. We make the rules.

An industry is made up of organizations. Who works in those organizations? People, like you and me. Everything comes down to people. If we're not changing our leadership structures, making room for more diversity, then we're just going to perpetuate bad practices.

My personal charge is to improve the diversity at my own firm, first.

I have connected with universities and the National Association of Minority Architects to develop a stronger pipeline of diverse candidates. I don't want to be in a position where I haven't done my part to create a flow of résumés from a diverse group of people. In my organization, we're doing good work, but we can do much more to lift others. It's an ongoing push to make our firm more diverse, representative and inclusive.

I often ask myself, "What is my capacity to create change today?" I encourage you to empower yourself by asking yourself the same daily question. What can you change today? That is your legacy.

WHEN LEGACY BUILDING IS A ROCKY ROAD

Here's a caveat—I want to be real about this. Leadership is messy and complicated. Not every person in an organization will buy into your vision. They won't always appreciate the legacy you're trying to build or want to be a part of it.

There have been times in my experience when employees have pushed back or wanted different things than what the company is offering, and those moments have sometimes made me question what the other leaders and I are trying to build. When people don't appreciate or understand the generous environment we're creating in our organization, that's really tough. When that happens, I admit that I feel the natural human impulse to just take care of myself. But I have to shake it off, reset and tune back into the vision. I have to remember that we're creating something new at Mancini and we're not going to get constant buy-in from everyone, every step of the way. There will always be realignments.

My Mancini partners and I want to create a workplace that is different from the status quo. We want a workplace where we truly care about employees and take care of everyone, not just the people at the top. We're building it together. When my partners and I retire, we want to look back and be proud of our legacy, of how people worked at the firm under our leadership, and know we're leaving the firm better than we found it.

And part of building something new is getting used to handling feedback and criticism about that new way of thinking. It's easy to have an emotional response to criticism, but to be true leaders, we need to listen openly and keep realigning our focus on the vision.

My vision for my impact organizations

With **SheBuildsMoney**, one of my key goals is to empower small business owners. In my industry, I've seen professionals who naturally understand design, but find running their business much harder. I want to empower those people to run successful, profitable firms.

With **SheBuildsWaves**, I want to help women build their careers boldly and authentically. We can all be trailblazers and every woman has the ability to make an impact. Even if you're not in a leadership role, speaking on stages or writing a book, you have the opportunity to talk to the woman next you, make a difference in someone's life and apply the mindset of always lifting others.

I would love to see SheBuildsWaves expand beyond the built industry. It already attracts people from outside of architecture and design, and I'd like to continue to grow its impact and create the strong community that women need when they're navigating their careers.

With **SheBuildsLives,** my dream is one day to open multiple free learning centers in low-income communities across Nigeria. I want to continue to provide resources and opportunities for these children so that they can actually believe in their dreams.

It's difficult to be a child in that country right now, living under an oppressive government. But education opens doors for children who are starting life at a disadvantage. If SheBuildsLives can give these kids a step up or provide a more level playing field, they can have a shot at a better life.

Your legacy has already started. You're living it right now. As you look forward at the impact you can make and the steps you can take in the future, remember always to be B.O.L.D.

BEING B.O.L.D.

Be yourself
Start with the values and goals that are most important to you. Your legacy is your integrity and only you can define those terms.

Open your mind to new definitions and opportunities
Stay flexible and open to the journey. You can't know now exactly how your legacy will play out. Slow down when you need to reassess your progress and look for new opportunities to create big, bold change.

Lift others
If you take one thing away from this book, I hope that it's this: our most important legacy is making an impact beyond ourselves. Your career does not have to be just about making money and advancing yourself. You have ample opportunities to serve and lift others along the way. When you lift others, you lift yourself.

Don't wait—do it now
Your legacy starts now. Don't wait for the end of your career to consider how you want to be remembered. Take small steps every day. I believe in you!

10
How To Be A B.O.L.D. Leader

I've talked a lot so far about how to boldly grow your career, push into your potential and make new rules, but once you get into a leadership position, how do you apply these same principles? How can you be yourself, open your mind, lift others and act with urgency?

Let's think about how to apply the B.O.L.D. framework to your role as a leader, based on how I have developed my own leadership philosophy.

Be yourself

When I think about how I show up as a leader, these are the questions I ask myself:

- How can I truly be myself, even when I'm in a leadership position?

- How can I act out **my** version of leadership, instead of the old ideas of what a leader "should" be?

- How can I craft a new definition of what a leader should do and be?

You could read a million leadership books and they would all give you a different idea of what a "leader" should be. The way I have experienced leadership, and the way I hope we can all start to think about leadership, is that it nurtures the people being led.

Once you're in a leadership position, your role is to make sure the folks that are under you are truly pushing into their maximum potential. They need to see you as someone who supports them in their career journey and helps them see what is possible. Your job isn't to give orders. It's to provide guidance. As a leader, you walk side by side with the people you lead. You are with them on their journey.

As a leader, I ask myself, "How can I show people that what they want is attainable?" The answer is I start by being myself. When I am an empathetic, authentic, approachable leader, people are able to connect with me and relate to me. They see a leader who is not just doing things according to the status quo—instead, I'm being Bolanle. I'm being myself, not someone else's idea of a leader.

At the heart of this idea is a simple truth: we're all human. We all have insecurities. Everyone's still figuring it all out. It's important that as a leader, while we're in the position of guiding and nurturing people, we also show them our human side.

My advice is to lean into who you are. Be yourself. Create an environment where employees can connect with you. Being bold means showing your human side, and in turn allowing others to show theirs and be themselves.

One interesting benefit of being real as a leader is that I've been able to quickly understand my own strengths and work on my weaknesses. When I show up as myself, I'm able to tap into my strengths, and tap into other people's strengths to complement mine. When they see me acknowledging and working on my weaknesses, they feel comfortable speaking up about the areas where they need help. The result is a stronger organization where everyone leans into their strengths and can really shine.

Open your mind to new
definitions and opportunities

Building a different kind of organization won't happen overnight, but as a leader, you can start with your team. Even if you can't steer your whole firm right now, how can you create an environment with your immediate team where people feel receptive to change? Open your mind to change and thinking about new ways your team could be run. If people on your team want to change the way things have always been done, challenge the status quo and set new definitions at work, are you receptive as a leader? Are you listening?

Once I decided to lead my team with that kind of open mind, we started working more effectively. When I look at my broader firm, the teams that have been most successful are led by people who are leaning into new ways of working. They're sharing financial information with their team, tying everyone's work to a bigger vision and coming to their people for ideas about how to improve. That open mindset leads to teams that are focused and working together.

Over my career, I've seen that the teams that don't perform as well are run by leaders who are stuck in old ways. They don't listen to their team's ideas and suggestions. That disconnect creates tension that trickles down into people's work. Employees show up to do their job and earn their paycheck, but they're stressed and tired.

Good leaders don't all lead in the same way, but they do understand the importance of being open minded. If you want to lead boldly, take a look at what is working in your organization. Which teams are running effectively? Then get to the foundation of what is making things work so well for them. Look at whether you could model parts of their way of working in your own team.

This is what I mean by creating a new definition. Scrap the old ways that aren't working, find what *does* work in your organization, and figure out how to replicate that model and put your own spin on it.

At an organizational level, you can enjoy success by rethinking old definitions. At Mancini, instead of building our firm to emulate traditionally successful names, we have leaned into what makes us unique and different, and we keep doing more of that. Just because other people are running their organization in a certain way doesn't mean we have to do the same. It's actually what we do *differently* that makes us stronger.

That's bold leadership: setting a new vision, not listening too much to the naysayers, focusing on your people and how you can be successful together, and bringing everyone along with you. If you need guiding words for this approach to leadership, remember *flexibility* and *innovation*. Making big changes means being flexible enough to let go of the old ways, and being excited about and open to innovative new ideas.

A NEW OPPORTUNITY FOR MY TEAM

Here's an example of a new way of working that has benefited my team of project accountants at Mancini.

In the past, project accountants didn't have much contact or relationship with the project managers. At Mancini, we saw an opportunity for the accountants to feel more involved and understand more about the projects they're working on, so we introduced a monthly financial review meeting with each project manager where we walk through the financial health and profitability of their projects. I spent six months as part of those meetings, and then I pulled myself out and let the project accountants lead their own meetings.

After we'd put this new opportunity in place, a project accountant on my team sent me a note saying that she really appreciated it as it allowed her to understand and enjoy her work in a new way. The subsequent improved relationships between the accountants and project managers help the firm as a whole run more successfully. As a leadership team, my partners and I are leaning into people's strengths, giving them a voice, then getting out of their way and letting them shine.

FOCUS ON THE WINS

If you're looking for a new way to make big decisions at your organization, try focusing on the wins. At Mancini, I have seen the value of taking time to reflect on what's working.

At our quarterly board meetings, we ask, "What is working for our clients, our projects and our people?" We dig a little deeper to understand what made each of those wins happen. Then we ask, "How can we do more of that in the next quarter?"

In our employee town halls, we communicate those wins to the people who made them happen.

If you're a bold leader, you're always looking for an opportunity to reinforce the value your team is bringing.

Lift others

Part of being open to new definitions and opportunities is being willing to give others the space to experiment, make mistakes and learn. That's how you lift people up—by letting them take ownership of their work and grow. If you think about it, that is a huge gift that many people never have during their careers. It's a focus on developing the people, not just the tasks that have to get done.

RESPECT EMPLOYEES' STRENGTHS AND GOALS

Here's an example from my firm. One of our project managers recently resigned, and we needed to fill their role. A junior employee (let's call her Ashley) who was usually very quiet at work came to the leadership team and volunteered to move into the job. She had a conversation with us about her goals, what she wanted to learn and what she thought she could bring to the role. We gave her the opportunity to step up.

We respected Ashley's strengths and goals. She was taking ownership of her career path, and we wanted to do everything we could to support her on that path, even if it meant giving her an opportunity to stretch beyond what she already knew. We assigned an internal mentor to help her and supported her when she wanted to apply to an emerging leadership program to grow her skills and network with others outside the organization. She's doing very well, challenging herself, learning and growing into the role.

Bold leaders also help employees learn about themselves.

A JOURNEY OF LEARNING

Years ago, I hired someone (let's call her Emily) who was strong in accounting, but I quickly saw that she had other skillsets hidden within her. It was important to me to empower her to explore different areas.

HOW TO BE A B.O.L.D. LEADER

Over the years, she has gotten the chance to try HR, operations and accounting. I've also made sure she knows that she can use her voice. I encourage her to speak up and tell me when she enjoys a new task or experience, or when she is struggling. We regularly talk about how we can craft her path to move her into the kinds of work she wants to do.

Just as I was open to various paths early in my career, I want to be open to the various paths in front of my team members and help them test out their options.

It's incredibly exciting as a leader to see people discover new possibilities, unlock their confidence and lean into their potential to learn what they can accomplish. Watching people become more effective and more keyed into their own strengths and the strength of the organization makes me feel like I'm doing something right as a leader.

That's how you lift others—you look for the potential in them, give them the support they need and help them step into new opportunities.

Don't wait—do it now

If you've ever wanted to lead boldly, the time is now.

I'll say that again. If you've ever wanted to lead boldly, the time is now.

Why not now? Time is going to pass anyway. If there are changes you want to make to your team, new ways of working you want to try, old rules you want to break, growth you want to reach for, new outcomes you want to see—do it now. Don't wait.

Make the changes you want to see little by little. If you can't change the whole firm, start on your team. Experimenting with change will only lead to you learning and growing as a leader. You have to start by taking a bold step now. If you wait for the perfect situation, you'll never find it.

My experience of leading a team and an organization through major internal changes and a global pandemic has shown me that if we had waited to make difficult decisions, we would have tolerated conditions that were detrimental to the organization. Bold leaders take risks. If you want to push your organization in a new direction, you have to be willing to take risks. Don't be afraid of the unknown. Don't stay stuck. Test fresh, new ideas and don't be afraid of failing.

Not every idea will work. At Mancini, we've rolled out tests and some have failed. When this happens, we are flexible. We ditch that idea and move on to the next one with a better understanding of what we need to succeed. Failures are merely learning opportunities to find out more about what will and won't work in our organization.

TRUST YOUR GUT

I'm a numbers person, so naturally I don't like the word "risk" when it comes to my company's financials. To me, smart risks are mitigated risks, but I've learned from my experience as a leader that we have to use two different elements when we make big decisions: the quantitative (the data) and the qualitative (our intuition, gut and the trust we have in the others on our team).

When my leadership team and I make decisions based on both the data and our guts, they usually pan out. However, when we make decisions based on just the data, we're missing an important element of decision making. We don't take the risk because it doesn't look perfect on paper, or we don't consider the full scope of the decision.

I've learned about this dual decision making from the president of Mancini. Even hiring me was a risk. On paper, I didn't have the perfect experience and qualifications, but he knew me, he saw that I could lean into my skills and he trusted that I could grow into the job. I've seen many lovely decisions like that one pay off for the firm. He has passed on that perspective to me, and now I'm more open to taking risks because I understand the numbers **and** the nuance.

His bold leadership has given me the freedom to be a bold leader.

My leadership challenge to you

Take your position and run with it. Implement good change.

We spend so much time at work. When you're in a position of leadership, you have a responsibility to create a work environment that positively impacts the lives of your employees.

Ask yourself:

- Am I creating an experience for employees that's **better** than what I came up through?

- Am I doing things because they have always been done that way, or am I pushing into **changes** that will make things better?

- Am I **listening** to my people and making them feel seen, heard and valued?

- Am I creating a culture that fosters **boldness**?

- What intentional **choices** will I make today?

And the most important question I ask myself every day:

Am I nurturing the people around me?

Conclusion

I have to be honest: when I first thought about writing a book, I was terrified. I'm a huge supporter of learning something new and changing my mind, so putting my current ideas down in words in something as permanent as a book seemed counterintuitive. What if I take a different path after the book is published? What if the organizations I've started change form, or die out all together?

But eventually, I realized that none of those possibilities mattered because I have written this book for *you*. We're building our playbooks together as we go. You're a part of my journey now.

What really matters is what you gain from reading this book, and what I have gained from the experience of writing it. The book itself is just one example of me being open to new opportunities, planting seeds and living as my authentic self to lift others right now. You'll always gain something when you bet on yourself. However, if you second-guess yourself or question whether you're making the right decision, you'll hold yourself back from making that impact. If you don't jump, you won't get hurt—but you'll also never fly.

When I look back at how my playbook has evolved to get me to today, I can see two themes.

First, the journey wasn't a straight path. There were always multiple paths in front of me, and I could only grow by being flexible and open to exploring those paths. It was important not to box myself into one vision, because I would have missed opportunities along the way.

Second, when I look back, I can see my moments of boldness. I see my courage growing over time. I see how my curiosity served me and opened doors. When I allowed myself to take the first step, I always found an educational moment: I learned about myself or where I wanted to go.

And I see how the B.O.L.D. framework has truly gotten me to where I am.

What I hope for you

- I hope you have the confidence to trust yourself.

- I hope you listen to your wildest ideas.

- I hope you go for it.

- I hope you show up as yourself.

- I hope you push aside the fears that are holding you back.

- I hope you let go of your limiting beliefs.

- I hope you practice courage and build your boldness muscle.

- I hope you make new rules for yourself and the people who depend on you.

- I hope you have the courage to build the work environment you've always wanted for yourself, and share that reality with others.

- I hope you try something new and forget the status quo.

- I hope you are flexible when things go wrong and bounce back up again. You'll figure it out and move forward.

- I hope you find your community, because none of us can go on this journey alone. If you're already in a community, I hope you become more active and inspire others.

- I hope you question your mindset about your own playbook. Remember that your legacy is in the present tense. It starts now. Is what you're doing **right now** supporting the legacy you want to build?

- I hope you think intentionally about your interactions and relationships. You never know who is going to come back around later in life.

- I hope you are an active participant in your career path, instead of letting your career happen to you.

- I hope you look back at the end of your career and feel fulfilled.

- I hope you design the life you want.

IT'S YOUR TURN

At the beginning of this book, I promised I'd give you the tools and frameworks to build boldly, craft your unique path and lead with courage. Now it's your turn. How can you apply my experiences and the frameworks I've shared to your career and life? How can this book apply to your unique situation?

- How can you **be yourself?**
- How can you **open your mind to new definitions and opportunities?**
- How can you **lift others?**
- How can you **do it now and stop waiting?**

Take what you've learned here and **run** with it!

B.O.L.D. Bonus: Ten prompts to help you build boldly

As you reflect on the lessons you've taken from this book, ask yourself hard questions about your own unique path. I've written ten prompts to get you started. Use these prompts in your own self-reflection, with reading groups and in your team at work.

1. **Be open to many paths.** What new opportunities could you watch out for? How could you boldly step into a new path, even if it's not the one you'd expected or planned for?

2. **Push into your potential.** How could you set yourself up to succeed in the next few months? Could you advocate for yourself? Ask for specific support, training or mentorship? Look at where you want to go and define the resources you need to get there.

3. **The power of visibility.** How could you boldly step into the spotlight—right now as who you really are? Could you raise your hand for the next opportunity at work? Could you finally lead the project you've had your eye on? How can you step up as your authentic self?

4. **Find your courage.** Do you have the courage to begin? Look for ways you could take the first step toward a big goal. Find little ways to flex your courage muscle, build your confidence and make progress toward your bold vision.

5. **Make new rules.** What is one old rule you're ready to break? If there's an "old way of doing things" that doesn't work for you, it's time to create a better way. Set your sights on that new, bold way of working. Then start talking about it. Bring people along with you.

6. **Transparency** leads to new connections and new opportunities. If you have been afraid to share your authentic story, start practicing now. How could you be more transparent at work, with your family, in your friend group or online? Practice sharing openly and you'll get more comfortable over time.

7. **Be generous.** Everyone has a role to play in helping others. Who could you lift up? Who could you mentor or advise? How could you share your time and energy? How could you give

to others? Start giving now and you'll be pushing yourself into your full potential and others into theirs.

8. **Build community.** How could you build a community where it doesn't exist already? How could you bring people together across traditional boundaries? What communities do you wish **you'd** had, and how could you build them now?

9. **Your legacy starts now.** You're building your legacy every day. It's about the little things. To build that legacy, you might need to "slow down to speed up." Pause and do a check-in with yourself. Are you still on track to where you want to go? What's slowing you down?

10. **How to be a B.O.L.D. leader.** As a leader, how can you actively nurture the people around you? What steps can you take to create an environment where employees can connect with you and be themselves?

I'd love to hear from you. How are you building boldly, charting your unique path and leading with courage? How has the B.O.L.D. framework unlocked new opportunities for you?

Please send me your stories—on social media with the hashtag #myBOLDpath, or by sending me a message via www.BolanleWO.com.

Acknowledgements

Thank you to God, who has blessed and called me to be B.O.L.D.

Deepest appreciation to my husband and partner in life, Temie. Your overwhelming support every single step of the way, especially encouraging me when it was time to write this book, has been exceptional. To my two incredible children, Teniola and Tsola. You are my reasons for making sure I live a B.O.L.D. life—so you can do even more in yours.

To my mother, Amudatu Beauty Amoda, thank you for being the blueprint and ensuring I got the best of your abilities. I am forever grateful.

To my best friend, Nosa Adetiba, thank you for being a constant and my biggest cheerleader. I'm blessed to have you encouraging me in all chapters of life. To Kunbi Odubogun, my friend and Building B.O.L.D. partner, who encouraged me to write this book and supported me on the journey. To Ugonna Ibe-Ejiogu, my friend, connector and all-around strategist. We did it! After many years of the push, the book has been realized.

Thank you to my partners, Christian Giordano, William Mandara, Scott Harrell, Jessica Mann-Amato and the Mancini Duffy family, for your continued support. To Patrick Kinsler, my first boss. You helped me build my career foundation. To Ted Maziejka, my mentor who helped me excel in my first year in a leadership position at Mancini.

To the team at Rethink Press for making this book come to life. To my community near and at large. You've all pushed me into my potential.

The Author

Bolanle Williams-Olley is the CFO and part-owner at Mancini Duffy, a technology-first design firm based in New York City. She is a dynamic leader within the built industry and is the founder of several impact organizations: SheBuilds-Lives, a nonprofit that addresses the needs of children and improves the quality of education in low-income schools and communities in Nigeria; SheBuildsMoney, an initiative that empowers small design firms to be successful and thrive financially; SheBuildsWaves, an organization designed to help women in the built industry find fulfillment in their roles by engaging and striving for more, together; and R.E.A.C.H. Nigeria, a connector hub that creates awareness about non-governmental organizations and volunteer opportunities across Nigeria.

Before her current position at Mancini Duffy, Bolanle served five years as a senior project accountant at Skidmore, Owings & Merrill and five years as a project accountant at HLW. She holds a master's degree in education and social policy from NYU, a master's degree in applied mathematics and a bachelor's degree in mathematics from the City University of New York, Hunter College.

She lives in New Jersey with her husband and two kids and is absolutely obsessed with throwing themed parties.

Connect with Bolanle via her website:

⊕ www.BolanleWO.com

Made in the USA
Middletown, DE
14 July 2022

69357876R00096